Improving Literacy Achievement

An Effective Approach to Continuous Progress

Carolyn E. Haley

LIBRARY
FRANKLIN PIERCE COLLEGE
RINDGE, NH 03461

Rowman & Littlefield Education
Lanham, Maryland • Toronto • Plymouth, UK

Published in the United States of America
by Rowman & Littlefield Education
A Division of Rowman & Littlefield Publishers, Inc.
A wholly owned subsidary of The Rowman & Littlefield Publishing Group, Inc.
4501 Forbes Boulevard, Suite 200, Lanham, Maryland 20706
www.rowmaneducation.com

Estover Road
Plymouth PL6 7PY
United Kingdom

Copyright © 2007 by Carolyn E. Haley

All rights reserved. No part of this publication may be reproduced,
stored in a retrieval system, or transmitted in any form or by any
means, electronic, mechanical, photocopying, recording, or otherwise,
without the prior permission of the publisher.

British Library Cataloguing in Publication Information Available

Library of Congress Cataloging-in-Publication Data
Haley, Carolyn E., 1949–
    Improving literacy achievement : an effective approach to continuous
progress / Carolyn E. Haley.
        p.   cm.
    Includes bibliographical references.
    ISBN-13: 978-1-57886-568-0 (hardback : alk. paper)
    ISBN-10: 1-57886-568-9 (hardback : alk. paper)
    ISBN-13: 978-1-57886-569-7 (pbk. : alk. paper)
    ISBN-10: 1-57886-569-7 (pbk. : alk. paper)
    1. Language arts (Primary)—United States. 2. Literacy programs—United
States. 3. School improvement programs—United States. I. Title.
    LB1529.U5H35 2007
    372.6—dc22   2006032201

∞™ The paper used in this publication meets the minimum requirements of
American National Standard for Information Sciences—Permanence of
Paper for Printed Library Materials, ANSI/NISO Z39.48-1992.
Manufactured in the United States of America.

Contents

Preface

The last ten years have brought sweeping changes and reforms in public education. Public education is what shapes our nation. Literacy achievement is always at the forefront as a measure of how well our education system is progressing. There is constant research on best practices and reform movements for improving literacy learning. When new reading and language programs surface, each is individually marketed as the one effective approach for literacy achievement. Educators looking for a quick fix often rush into purchasing and implementing these new programs. As a seasoned educator, I find that many new programs and practices are short-lived because educators are looking for quick fixes. If you expect to have sustained results from a new literacy program, it is going to take a minimum of two years to prove effective. Quick fixes are quick to go. That is why you find school districts trying one program after another.

President George W. Bush and former president Bill Clinton are strong supporters of their education goals and beliefs. Two of the goals both presidents have put at the forefront are (1) every child will start school ready to learn and (2) every child will read at or above grade level by third grade. A now-mandatory accountability for these two goals and others is the No Child Left Behind (NCLB) Act. The NCLB Act states that all children will demonstrate proficiency on state tests in reading and math by the 2013–2014 school year. If we want students to experience success throughout their school years, they must be literacy proficient. In order for students to pass state-mandated tests, they must be literacy proficient.

According to the NCLB Act, the first benchmark of accountability to demonstrate literacy proficiency occurs in third grade. With third grade as the initial benchmark, we as educators must provide literacy instruction that is intense, solid, and effective for student achievement in this discipline *before* they reach third grade. We are setting students up for failure when they are allowed to enter third grade significantly behind in literacy development. For example, when you have third-grade students whose reading performance is equivalent to first-grade skills (reading level 1.5) and they are administered a test with readability equivalent to 3.0 to 3.9, these students have failed before taking the test. How can we realistically expect students in third or even fifth grade to demonstrate literacy proficiency on grade level when they start that grade level lagging one to two years behind?

The primary instructional focus in the early grades is reading and math. Without mastery of literacy skills in the early grades, students will find themselves struggling in other subjects as they move into intermediate, middle, and high school. High-stakes testing as a result of the NCLB Act is showing some improvement in reading and math, but the improvement margin is narrow. With all the remedial best-practices research, innovative programs, and reform movements tried and or put in place by school divisions throughout our nation, you would think the improvement margin would be wider. In an article in *Education Week*, Olson reports a mixed picture of results: "While the data show similar upward trends since 2000 in both reading and math in grades fourth and eighth, they also show that progress has slowed in the past two years, when the NCLB Act might have been starting to have an impact" (2005, 22).

I predict that within the next two to three years we are going to face another education crisis. This crisis will show that our students are becoming *robotic* learners. As a seasoned school administrator with thirty-two years of experience in both suburban and urban schools as well as experience in other facets of education, I've seen innovative and instructional programs come and go. Educational programs seem to rotate on a cycle. My administrative experiences have broadened my perspective on which programs are likely to work for students and what may need to take a back seat. Every five years I change schools. I never wanted to be the school administrator who stayed at the same school for twenty to thirty years. Each school is different even though it is in the same district as another, and each school has its own unique challenges; however, literacy/reading is always the primary focus at the elementary school level, no matter what school or school district. In addition, changing schools allows one the opportunity to work with diverse groups of people, and to listen and learn from diverse ideas and beliefs is an experience in itself.

One major concern that I saw developing during my last two years as a school administrator is the negative impact that the NCLB Act is having on teachers, school administrators, and even district administrators. Lately, you don't hear as much controversy and criticism of the NCLB Act, nor are educators allowing themselves to become frustrated by the linear focus on mandated test results. Everyone realizes that this act is not going away anytime soon. As a covert reaction to what has been an overt reaction, many schools have settled into developing their instructional programs around only the skills needed to pass these mandated tests. Because of the linear focus on state testing, we have produced a linear curriculum for teachers to teach and administrators to monitor.

As a result, we will start producing robotic students. Every student is now receiving the same instruction within the same time frame. No consideration is given to individualization or innovativeness in teaching and learning. *A Nation at Risk* called for a national curriculum. Is this what the NCLB Act has become? I don't see how our nation can justify a national curriculum with as much diversity as we have within our population. How can we knowingly rule out the fact that people learn differently and at different levels? How are we addressing the specific needs of below average or slow learners, average learners, and above average or gifted learners?

It is ironic that what I see happening to instructional programs, Berliner and Biddle also reported:

> Teachers who work in schools subjected to such programs report that their worries about the school's status and the shallowness of accountability evaluations consume their time and energy. Over time, these programs tend to generate the three A's, Anxiety, Anger, and Alienation. Teachers feel anxious when their schools face accountability systems, especially systems that are imposed by higher authorities and that are used to make important decisions about their lives. They feel anger when they discover that those accountability systems are used unfairly—when they provide rewards or impose punishments on undeserving schools.
>
> And when teachers learn they have little ability to change unfair accountability systems, they become alienated, passive-aggressive members of the community, acting as obstructionists for other new ideas that come along. To say the least, this does not sound like a good recipe for improving American education. In response to these worries and pressures, educators also begin to adjust the focus of their efforts. Over time, their curricula and teaching efforts become more standardized and superficial. Moreover, since they want their schools to look good on competitive tests, they tend to restrict instruction to the topics assessed on those tests. (1995, 196)

As educational programs change, school districts continue to seek linear approaches to school reform. The idea of developing and implementing a continuous progress program as a means of maximizing literacy achievement in the primary grades (K–3) entails components from several research developments. The continuous progress program approach I developed and implemented calls for restructuring primary-grade designations into nongraded literacy skill levels. This approach to restructuring is nontraditional; therefore, to understand its concept, you must be able to think outside the box. The one area of the traditional primary program that doesn't change in this approach is the content of the literacy (reading/language) curriculum. This program is designed for intense literacy instruction matched to individual needs of students. Primary teachers experience a different conception of how to group students and teach literacy skills.

This approach truly embraces individualization as its main focus for literacy development. Literacy achievement is the primary focus, and literacy success is the expected result. Student data results from this program showed that 95 percent of primary students who completed the program demonstrated literacy proficiency at or above grade level by third grade.

What many will find hard to believe is the low budget needed to operate this program. I say "low budget" because the greatest expense will come from hiring qualified, committed teachers. When I speak of highly qualified teachers, I always include the word *committed* because you can hire certified teachers, but certification doesn't necessarily mean a person is committed to student success and achievement. When you compare salary cost to a single instructional program cost of $6 billion, this is low budget. Congress authorized $6 billion over six years for the Bush administration's flagship initiative to implement a program called Reading First (Manzo 2005, 22). I am amazed at the amount of state, federal, and local funding that has gone into literacy programs since the No Child Left Behind Act was passed, producing small marginal results.

Reading First is a packaged program, many of which have come and gone, with special materials, resources, and textbooks. Of course, unless you purchase the entire package, the program will not get you the benefits expected. Is this another Reading Recovery program that shows immediate progress but does not sustain it? Reading First is not without criticism from Robert Slavin, founder of Success for All, and the Reading Recovery Council, citing conflict of interest laws (Manzo 2005, 22).

With all the funding of, research on, and adoption of new costly literacy programs, Olson reports, "Based on the current rate of improvement on National Assessment of Educational Progress (NAEP), the NCLB Act's goal that all children will be proficient on state tests in reading and math by 2013–14 appears unlikely to be met, even assuming that what counts for proficient in many states is closer to NAEP basic achievement level. The proportion of students at or above basic inched up only a few percentage points, at most, between the 2003 and 2005 national assessments" (2005, 1). Margaret Spelling, secretary of education, states, "I think it does show us that we're going to need to accelerate our progress at all grade levels and with all kids if we're to meet goals. We actually won't do it, if we don't think we can do it" (Spelling 2005, 22).

I speak from my personal experience at the school and district levels when I say that billions upon billions of dollars have gone into responses to the NCLB Act. State, local, and federal monies have been poured into making students literacy proficient at the elementary level, and the results cannot begin to measure up. On the optimistic side, some progress is better than no progress.

OVERVIEW

This book focuses on improving literacy achievement through a continuous progress program approach. Throughout the past twenty years, educators have successfully and sometimes unsuccessfully tried research-based reading and language programs and practices. Many are recycled versions of once-tried programs wearing different hats as titles. Nevertheless, schools are continuously implementing new literacy/reading programs and models for all levels of performance.

My last school tried several programs before I came on board with my proposal to implement the continuous progress approach. I feel that this program is the most viable approach for our schools' literacy deficiencies. One of the programs previously tried was Reading Recovery. This is the program most schools in my district used to address literacy problems. It proved successful for schools in our suburban district that had small percentages of below average readers. However, for a school such as mine, with a high percentage of struggling readers and nonreaders, it did not prove effective. For example, a colleague from an affluent school in our district told me that he had about fourteen students in the entire school who were experiencing difficulty with literacy development. My school, on the other hand, had thirty-six or more students just from one grade level experiencing difficulty with literacy development.

One teacher in my school was trained for this process (the training cost is high, averaging $2,500 per person). The guidelines restricted use of the process by any person other than the one trained to use the program techniques. We had one teacher working one-on-one with students for six to eight weeks for forty-five minutes to an hour. I believe eight students were all she was able to work with during one school year. This small number of students was not going to impact or help our literacy deficiencies. What happened most often is that when a student exited this program and was placed back in his or her regular literacy instruction in the classroom, the student did not seem to maintain mastery of the reading strategies learned. There was no strong collaboration between the classroom and Reading Recovery teachers; therefore, a lack of instructional continuity occurred.

The whole-language approach was implemented prior to my tenure as well, and it was a disaster because the teachers were not trained; therefore, no one thoroughly understood the philosophy. The program faltered during implementation. Many students suffered setbacks due to a year of instructional floundering. Student data for that year reported deficiencies in phonics and comprehension. Success for All was tried as an alternative. While students showed some progress in reading, teachers were not consistent with the instructional focus of this program.

Students' low literacy achievement was not due to lack of trying to find new programs and practices but was due to a lack of common philosophies, techniques, training, and overall knowledge behind researching programs based on specific needs at the school site. As educators, we need to do more homework on researching best practices. Before we do so, we need to make certain that everyone is on the same page during development and implementation and that all are seeking the same outcome.

Buzzwords like *continuous improvement* are now surfacing, and this concept aligns with my continuous progress approach. As with most research and innovative literacy improvement programs, there has to be an introduction point. Critics' first comment about this program is that they have never heard of such a program for reading. Yet I believe the same comments were made about Reading Recovery, Success for All, whole language, multiage classrooms, differentiated learning, balanced literacy, and so forth, as each was introduced to the public. All these programs, along with my continuous progress approach, originated from necessity to improve student achievement and literacy.

The continuous progress program is designed to increase literacy achievement in the primary grades. The bell curve for our school looked upside down, with the majority of students' literacy performance at the lower end. I researched many programs, ideas, and methods but did not find one with every component we needed under one umbrella. Our school was in desperate need of a strong, solid alternative approach or program that would yield achievement results for our students. I was not looking for a quick fix but for a comprehensive approach that would be long lasting.

According to the achievement data, our school was the lowest-performing school of forty elementary schools at that time. The Iowa Test of Basic Skills was the state predictor used, with the second and fourth grades as benchmark grades. The results from this standardized test showed that over 40 percent of our 102 second-grade students scored in the bottom quartile in reading. In fourth grade, almost 35 percent of ninety students scored in the bottom quartile. As a result of the continuous progress approach to literacy achievement, my school went from being the lowest of forty elementary schools to placing in the top twenty-five. After our third year of implementation, the local news headline read, "Two Schools Hold Secret to SOL Test: Elementary Schools Recognized by Virginia Board for Improvements" (Forster 1999). My school was one of the two recognized.

Chapter 1 of this book defines continuous progress as an approach to literacy achievement. This chapter discusses its rationale and who would benefit from this type of nontraditional program. It emphasizes the difference between multiage classrooms and nongraded performance levels. It focuses on challenges encountered during the development and implementation stages.

Chapter 2 compares the structure of the continuous progress program to a traditional school program. Advantages and disadvantages are discussed. Performance grouping is defined and contrasted with ability grouping. Quarterly assessments used for student placement and instruction are presented. The fact that retention is no longer an alternative is discussed. The use of looping in intermediate grades (fourth and fifth) is looked at.

Chapter 3 examines the steps of restructuring a school for literacy achievement through the continuous progress program. This chapter discusses the roles of key people involved (principal, teachers, central office staff, parents, and students). It emphasizes the importance of establishing a school culture within the learning community. The importance of collaborative relations as a team approach is defined and discussed. Professional development is examined and implemented as a different model. This chapter presents all program components in operation, and it ends with a look at how looping addresses continuous progress in a different perspective.

Chapter 4 revisits the steps that should be taken to develop and implement an effective approach to continuous progress for a successful literacy achievement outcome.

Acknowledgments

I want to deeply thank Amy Marie White (former assistant principal) and Kris Pedersen (former associate superintendent) for their dedication and involvement in our program's success. Also, a special thanks to the teachers and staff of Triangle Elementary School, for their willingness, hard work, and dedication to make a difference. A special thank you goes out to Sandra Carrillo (assistant principal) for her support and hard work in maintaining the success of our literacy program.

Heartfelt thanks to my mother, Frankie Martin, who has always been by my side.

CHAPTER 1

What Is the Continuous Progress Approach?

DEFINING LITERACY

Literacy is always at the forefront of school improvement plans. In fact, most school reform movements are primarily to improve student achievement in literacy in elementary schools. Special projects and plans develop from middle and high schools to address this continuing decline in proficiency.

Joyce writes, "That an immense number of children do not learn to read and write effectively terrifies the public. The media loudly announce that sending children to school ensures real literacy for only two out of three, and the media have the facts straight on that aspect of the subject. Nearly everyone now acknowledges that the human costs of not attaining proficiency in literacy have been escalating, whether one considers quality of life, employability, or the national ability to cope" (1999, 663).

Today *literacy* is a word with multiple meanings. Its scope has broadened over the past several years. For example, we hear the word attached to emergent literacy, computer literacy, literacy instruction, and so forth. According to Sensenbaugh, "The definition of literacy has expanded well beyond that found in the scope note of the 1988 ERIC Thesaurus: 'Literacy is the ability to read and write to communicate with written or printed symbols.' Literacy involves making meaning from a variety of sources and communicating it to a variety of audiences" (1990, 2). I am sharing this definition as a more technical meaning of the word *literacy*. When I speak of literacy achievement in this book, I am referring to basic reading, writing, and vocabulary development. It is my belief that all three should be interwoven under the heading of literacy. And for all practical purposes, that is what is considered literacy achievement in my continuous progress approach.

As large and wealthy as our nation is, we continue to put strong emphasis on reading and writing development. As large and wealthy as our nation is, we continue to experience low performance in literacy proficiency.

More and more reading programs are surfacing, as are ideas about how to effectively approach the teaching of reading. Some work, and some don't. Our nation's literacy achievement has always been a focus for improvement, so much so that we are still looking for the clue to the high numbers of literacy-deficient people in our nation. Language impacts reading, reading impacts writing, and all three are what we use for communication. If we can assure student success and achievement in literacy development at an early age, then we can decrease illiteracy and hopefully decrease the school dropout rate. Students don't drop out because they are successful; they drop out because of a lack of success. That is why it is very important that our primary students become strong, literacy-proficient students and that they experience success and achievement in learning at a young age.

Sensenbaugh feels Graff's position on literacy may be the most constructive for the future: "What is needed is a broader view of reading and writing that integrates and emphasizes the many human abilities in a context of a changing world that requires their development and use. Paths to learning individual literacy by the young must be made less rigid; more attention must be paid to different sequences and structures of learning; and more sensitivity must be shown toward cultural and class influences" (Sensenbaugh, 1990, 2).

Teaching literacy disciplines (reading, writing, and vocabulary development) from a continuous progress approach can be unique in structure, but the results have closed achievement gaps and produced high achievement results in literacy for all students regardless of race, culture, and economic background.

WHAT IS CONTINUOUS PROGRESS?

The words *continuous progress* describe a framework for improving literacy achievement. It is a comprehensive program designed to increase student achievement in reading and language arts by identifying, through individual assessments, specific skill gaps in literacy. When students, especially those in the primary grades (K–3), experience gaps in literacy development, these gaps widen as they continue to go unfilled. As a result, students experience frustration and struggle to acquire success in literacy. Continuous progress is a conceptual approach designed to ensure literacy success for all students, including below average or slow learners, average learners, and above average learners.

According to Grant, Johnson, and Richardson, perhaps the most concise definition of *continuous progress practices* is the one written by Madeline Hunter, which explains the meaning in these terms: "Continuous progress refers to a student's progress from time of school entry until graduation. With continuous progress, students are challenged appropriately according to their ability to master intellectual, physical, emotional, and social tasks at progressively more difficult levels. Continuous progress mandates that students should neither spend time on what they have already adequately achieved, nor proceed to more difficult tasks if they have not yet learned materials or acquired skills essential to that new level of knowledge" (1996, 5).

The above definition looks at continuous progress from the time a student enters school to graduation. I look at continuous progress during the block of time when students are in the primary grades (K–3). Also, I focus on literacy development as a means to keep students from spending time on those literacy skills they have already mastered, and yet to prevent them from proceeding to more difficult tasks until they have learned the skills essential to that new level of knowledge.

The operative word in Hunter's definition is *progressively*. This is the overall contextual meaning of continuous progress as it relates to literacy achievement. Learning to read, write, and speak during the primary years in school should not be a struggle or frustrating for young children. The experience should be rewarding and exciting. When students feel good about learning, they become self-motivated to learn and do more. I can recall my experience as a primary teacher when students experienced that they could now read: their smiles extended from one side of their faces to the other.

Moustafa notes, "Learning to read should be a joyous adventure as exciting for youngsters, their families, and their teachers as when children learn to walk and talk. The key to making the journey a happy one is that we provide appropriate support" (1997, xiv).

NONGRADED VERSUS GRADED

The first time I proposed to develop a continuous progress approach as a school reform to improve literacy learning, the perception people had in mind was a multiage program, which was inaccurate. In my continuous progress approach, I recommended that we look at our primary-grade classes as nongraded in terms of designations such as first grade, second grade, and third grade, and that we replace grade designations by performance-based skill levels addressing literacy development. A continuous progress concept would allow the flexibility to do this, as it would give students the flexibility to move in and out of skill levels as their needs and mastery demonstrated. I knew the concept of a nongraded program was difficult for people to digest, so I shared what Anderson and Pavan listed as a brief operational definition of a nongraded school program:

1. Individual differences in the pupil population are accepted and respected, and there is ample variability in instructional approaches to respond to varying needs.
2. Learning, which is the "work" of the child, is intended to be not only challenging but pleasurable and rewarding.

3. Students are viewed as a whole; development in cognitive, physical, aesthetic, social, and emotional spheres is nurtured.
4. The administrative and organizational framework, for example with respect to pupil grouping practices, is flexible and provides opportunities for each child to interact with children and adults.
5. Students are enabled through flexible arrangements to progress at their own best pace and in appropriately varied ways. Instruction, learning opportunities, and movement within the curriculum are individualized to correspond with individual needs, interests, and abilities.
6. Curricular areas are both integrated and separate.
7. The expected standards of performance (in terms of outcomes) in the core areas of curriculum are clearly defined, so that the points to be reached by the end of a designated period are well known.
8. Within the curriculum and related assessment practices, specific content learning is generally subordinate to the understanding of major concepts and methods of inquiry and the development of the skills of learning.
9. Student assessment is holistic, to correspond with the holistic view of learning.
10. Evaluation of the learner is continuous, comprehensive, and diagnostic.
11. While there are some core components of the curriculum that are especially valued (as reflected in performance standards in the major content areas), the system is largely teacher managed and controlled. (1993, 62–63)

After I shared and expanded on the above areas, there was less of an amazed look on people's faces and more of a need to hear more information. Some were still trying to distinguish between the idea of multiage classrooms and the fact that some students would be assigned to skill levels by literacy strengths and needs rather than by age. Therefore, five- and six-year-olds could be together, six- and seven-year-olds could be together, and seven- and eight-year-olds could be together. A nongraded continuous progress approach would allow students to be placed in levels (classes) by literacy performance and not by age. See figure 1.1.

In the continuous progress approach, grade-level designations are removed and replaced by literacy performance levels clustered in teams. For example, team one has five levels (depending on the number of students at this range of performance). Students entering level 1 are usually those exiting kindergarten after one year but without mastery of the entire curriculum. For example, students may know 50 percent of letters and sounds. They do not need to go through another full year of kindergarten; they just need to continue where they left off the year before. Students in level 5 are also exiting kindergarten after one year and are well on their way in reading and writing skills. At the end of the school year, every student completes a writing sample and literacy as-

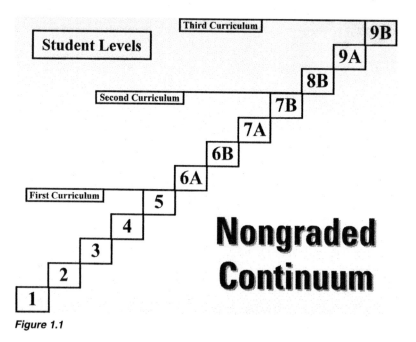

Figure 1.1

sessment. Below are end-of-school-year writing samples from three students who were in the same kindergarten class. Each student is placed at a different performance level for the upcoming school year.

Student A writes the following letters: FDOTOIKIT (no spacing). When asked to tell what the letters say, the student replies, "I went to Virginia Beach." This student is placed in level 1. The student can write letters but has no concept of sound and symbol. Student B writes, "L ephant p m up w h t." This student says that he wrote "The elephant picked me up with his trunk." This student is placed in level 2. The student has some concept of letter-sound symbols at the beginning of words and the concept of word order but needs more time to develop middle and ending sounds. Student C writes, "I am playing soccer with my friend." This student is placed in level 5. This student knows all letters and sounds, can spell adequately, can sequence, and can read what is written without prompting. As you can see, the range is wide between performance levels. Each example represents a level of students with similar performance.

According to Goodlad and Anderson,

> Children enter the first grade unit or first grade when they're approximately six years old, perhaps after completing a year of kindergarten. They, their parents and their teachers view the development of reading skills as a phenomenon that will occur soon after the children cross the school's magic threshold. Their expectations frequently turn to disillusionment. The realities of child development defy the rigorous ordering of children's abilities and attainments into conventional graded structure. For example, in the average first grade there is a spread of four years in pupil readiness to learn as suggested by mental age data. As pupils progress through the grades, the span in readiness widens. (1987, 3)

Continuous progress allows these students to be placed at literacy performance levels that match their needs. There are no grade designations to lock students into areas of learning that they have already achieved or to block them into areas of instruction that may be too difficult. Unlike the multiage classroom, which is developed by chance, the continuous progress approach is based on assessment data of individual performance levels.

When I say that multiage classrooms are developed by chance, it is usually because there are either too many or too few students in one or more grade levels to justify one graded class. For example, as a school year gets close to the end, principals begin to look at grade-level numbers for the upcoming school year. Let's say that in May, second-grade enrollment justifies three third-grade classrooms of twenty-five students for the upcoming year. The first-grade enrollment also justifies three second-grade classes of twenty-five students for the next school year. However, once school opens for the next school year, the principal finds that enrollment has changed for both grade levels. He or she now has fewer third-grade students; in fact, there are only enough students for two and a half classrooms (because any more students added to the other two classes will cause overcrowded conditions). As the principal looks at second-grade enrollment, he or she finds a similar situation: not enough students for three complete classes. Therefore, the principal makes an administrative decision to combine half a class of third-grade students with half a class of second-grade students to have a complete classroom. This is what constitutes a multiage classroom. Grant, Johnson, and Richardson write,

> A combination split/grade class often exists only for a one-year period. It is usually created for budgetary reasons or because there are too few students to justify two different classrooms. Staff in a combination or split grade report great difficulty teaching and managing two separate grade levels. A joint study by the Virginia Education Association and Appalachia Educational Laboratory notes, "The consensus on difficulties (experienced in combination grade classrooms) by 83 percent of the respondents can be capsulized in the response double teaching, double planning, double grading, and double record keeping."(1996, 7)

In comparison, with the continuous progress program you may have some five- and six-year-olds together at a level, and you may have six- and seven-year-olds and seven- and eight-year-olds together, not by chance but by performance levels. The placement of these students is based on individual development in literacy skills. There are no rigid grade designations for our primary students. Initially, traditional grade-level designations in the continuous progress program did not begin until fourth grade, but when the NCLB Act came into effect, we had to begin traditional grade-level designations in third grade. The hierarchy of literacy levels on the continuous progress continuum is seamless and moves upward in difficulty of literacy skills. The ultimate goal is for all students to demonstrate literacy proficiency at or above grade level by the time each one reaches level 8 on the continuum.

According to figure 1.1, the levels range from 1 to 9. Level 8 is equivalent to a reading level of 3.1. Students do not speak of grade levels as their placement; they say, "I am in Mrs. Smith's class." Continuous progress is flexible, and students are not locked into or tracked on a certain performance level. Ongoing quarterly assessments and evaluations allow students to show mastery every six to eight weeks and move from one level to another midyear (January) and at the end of the school year (June). Therefore, every student has the opportunity to move forward at least twice within a school year. Even though the reorganization of the primary classes is unique, the content of the reading and language arts curriculum remains the same. What is different is the scope and sequence of the curriculum. Literacy skills are chunked and sequenced by levels of advancement.

For example, students in levels 1 and 2 (six-year-olds) continue the kindergarten curriculum where they left off the year before. Students (also six-year-olds) in levels 3, 4, and 5 receive literacy instruction in first-level reading and language arts skills; however, each level consists of instruction from a different sequence of the curriculum. For example, students in levels 1 and 2 may begin instruction with long and short vowels. Students in level 3 have already mastered these skills, and students at this level may begin with nouns, verbs, and consonant-vowel-consonant patterns, while students in level 5 are introduced to adjectives and prefixes. These examples show how teachers on the same team do not start instruction in the same place within the curriculum even though their students are the same age and have had the same formal experience in the school setting.

Where each teacher on a team begins his or her instruction depends on student data for the level (class). Students' placement at each level is based on literacy assessments. Therefore, a primary component of the continuous progress approach is performance grouping. Performance grouping allows teachers to effectively plan literacy instruction to meet individual needs. Within the traditional classroom, primary teachers have to develop literacy plans for an average of five to six performance groups. Most of a primary teacher's instructional day is spent rotating from one reading group to another while planning for independent seatwork for the other groups. Teachers feel stressed from all the different levels of planning involved. In addition, with so many different performance groups come different textbooks and materials. Teachers are loaded down with various levels of reading texts. This affects instructional planning and teaching. Can you imagine how effective literacy instruction is for the last group of the day?

The continuous progress approach is based on the premise that students should not waste valuable instructional time on what they have already mastered, nor should students be allowed to continuously progress to skill areas that are more difficult if they have not yet mastered skills essential to success in new learning. As Gaustad writes, "Although nongraded education can be used by all ages, it is particularly appropriate during the primary years, when developmental differences are greatest. Children move from easy to difficult material at varying rates of speed, making continuous progress rather than being promoted once per year. Curriculum and teaching practices are developmentally appropriate, and an integrated curriculum seeks to foster children's physical, social, and emotional growth along with their intellectual growth" (1992b, 2).

For example, a school has 110 kindergarten students enrolled. The range in performance at entrance is wide. At the end of the school year, thirty-two of these same kindergarten students are recommended for retention due to very low literacy development. Due to parental rejection of retention at the kindergarten level, these students are promoted to first grade. When kindergarten students lacking appropriate literacy skills enter first grade, the first-grade teacher has to drop back to get these students caught up. At the same time, first-grade teachers are responsible for instruction of other students in the class who are ready for first-grade literacy instruction. When first-grade teachers have to teach kindergarten skills, there is not much time left for teaching first-grade skills; therefore, second-grade teachers end up dropping back their instruction to teach first-grade skills, and the domino effect goes on throughout the grade levels.

By the time students reach fifth grade, many are far behind in literacy learning because the gap widens as students continue to move forward lacking proficiency in skills they should know. During my first year as principal at Triangle Elementary School, thirty-two of our sixty-five fifth-grade students were promoted to middle school (sixth grade) with literacy skills that were two to three years behind, which put them behind in subject areas such as social studies and science. Middle school teachers and administrators felt frustration because their school had to provide remedial programs in literacy and tutorial programs for other core subjects. As parents and educators, we must take seriously the fact that student success in the primary grades is crucial for future success and achievement throughout later years in school.

UNDERSTANDING THE RATIONALE

The primary rationale for implementing the continuous progress approach was to improve literacy achievement in the primary grades (K–3). While this reform movement focused on the primary grades, the intent was to improve literacy achievement in all grades at the elementary level (K–5). Research and my own personal experience in education tell us that when students in primary grades struggle with reading and never receive the support and instruction they need to be successful in overcoming literacy deficiencies, they will continue to struggle and remain behind in the intermediate grades and throughout their school years. The students in Triangle Elementary School were in grave need of help with literacy achievement. Over 50 percent of students at any one grade level were either at or below the twenty-fifth percentile in reading performance.

Upon my being hired as principal, the superintendent made it clear that this school was in need of serious academic help. He alerted me that the test scores were very low, discipline was out of control, and there was a lack of instructional focus. I did not want to go into this school with the thought that maybe the teachers were not good teachers because quite often that is not the case. Nor did I want to go into the school with the thought that the students couldn't learn. Therefore, I focused on what was happening with the instructional program. Was the current program meeting the needs of the students? The reading curriculum was the same across the district. Students were using the same basal readers as other students across the district. My classroom observations noted teachers teaching from the basal reader.

Then why were so many students struggling with reading at their expected grade levels? In one of the second-grade classrooms, I observed the teacher teaching a small group of students in reading. The group was engaged in round-robin reading (an undesirable task). I noticed several students flipping pages, not on task or on the correct page. The student reading was stumbling through words, which lead me to believe she had no background using word attack skills. As you can imagine, the entire reading lesson was uneventful for all. As I continued to visit classrooms, I entered a fifth-grade classroom where the teacher was instructing the whole group in an English lesson. As I entered, she was reprimanding a student for exhibiting inappropriate behavior and disturbing classroom instruction.

I focused on this particular student after entering and watched him trying to complete a worksheet as the teacher instructed. He seemed to be writing answers randomly without reading what was on the paper. I walked over to stand beside the young man to see what he was writing. I could see that his context-clue answers were incorrect. I quietly bent over and asked the young man to erase his answers and start over again and focus on reading the sentences. He smiled and nodded in agreement. After leaving this classroom and returning to my office, I decided to ask the second-grade teacher to send me one of her students and asked that the student bring his or her reading text. Then I asked the fifth-grade teacher to have her young man come to my office with the worksheet he had been asked to complete.

When the second-grader came, I assured her that everything was all right; I was just interested in listening to her read a paragraph for me. The student turned to the story they were working on in class. I was stunned to hear her stumble over words and omit or say words in a way that made no sense in the context of the paragraph. This was a second-grade student in a second-grade basal reading book.

I thanked her warmly and had her return to class while the fifth-grade student entered my office. I gave him the same warm welcome to let him know there was no problem with him. I pointed to an incomplete sentence on his worksheet and asked him to read it for me. He knew the first word but stumbled through the rest of the sentence. It appeared to me that he was inattentive and causing disturbance because he could not keep up with what he was supposed to do and could not read the material well. I also concluded that students were flipping through their reading text in second grade because the student reading was having difficulty and that took away from the group's understanding of the paragraph. Also, there were several other students in the group with the same reading difficulty.

What I concluded from additional observations and monitoring of literacy instruction in the building is that students were in their correct grade-level classes according to age and were given instruction, materials, and resources according to their grade levels, but their actual reading performance levels were below their grade levels. Teachers knew this but struggled with the fact that this problem impacted more than half of each class; therefore, the question became whether to go back and instruct students on previous grade-level skills or keep pushing and struggling with students to go through grade-level instruction that they were not prepared for or developmentally ready to pursue. I was able to extrapolate from classroom data that there was a wide range of student performance levels in all classrooms and that to teach and plan for all these different levels was not going to be effective.

In any one first-grade classroom, there were students ranging from the first to ninety-ninth percentiles in reading development. This same range of performance was noted in all classes. As stated earlier, the premise of continuous progress acknowledges that every child is different and unique in his or her development. All students of the same age are not going to be at the same level of development, and we have to work with students according to where they are and use this as a means of providing the skills and knowledge they need to progress forward and feel successful in their performance. Success yields self-motivation. When students are self-motivated, they push themselves forward and are able to grasp more than they would if they lacked the motivation to learn.

Therefore, the most logical and innovative approach to increasing literacy achievement at this site was to remove grade-level barriers that dictated school curriculums by age, which is a cookie-cutter approach to learning instead of instructing students according to their developmental readiness as independent learners. Primary students especially will benefit from removal of grade-level barriers because the early grades are where you find wide ranges of student performance levels. I decided to look at literacy instruction (reading, writing, and vocabulary development) as a hierarchy of skill levels, not attaching grade levels to the skill areas but looking at them as a means of developmental progression. In doing so, I was able to show how the continuous progress model can present the literacy skill levels in a continuum format that classifies them into stages of developmental growth.

Vygotsky's zone of proximal development supports my rationale for literacy achievement through the continuous progress approach. According to Au, Carroll, and Scheu, Vygotsky states,

> The learning the child is doing, or the new level of performance the child is attempting, must be in the zone of proximal development. Below the zone, the child will not learn anything new, because the level of performance is too easy. Beyond the zone, the child will not benefit either, because the level of performance demanded is too difficult. To help the child learn, the teacher or peer must engage him in a performance of just the right degree of difficulty. (1997, 15)

School Board Waiver

There is a policy in our school district that anytime a school is interested in making instructional changes outside traditional policy, the school administrator must request a waiver from the school board. I presented to the school board my proposal to develop and implement a continuous progress approach to increase literacy achievement. The information needed for the waiver request included rationale, impact, goal statement, program development, tentative implementation plan, and outcome measures. The rationale and goal statements below are what I wrote for the school board waiver.

> Rationale: Triangle Elementary School faces two major challenges. First, our mobility index is the highest in Prince William County, averaging 38 percent. (It is important to note that this is not a result of our proximity to Quantico Marine Base. Less than 2 percent of our students are from military families.) A second major concern is the fact that, according to standardized test data, more than two-thirds of our students remain in the bottom quartile at second and fourth grade. In addition, less than one-third are in the top quartile. This is a pattern of long standing at Triangle. Implementation of a nongraded continuous progress program will allow us to assign students to classes designed to meet their individual needs.

The high percentage of our learners who require the time and intense instruction at their developmental level in order to narrow this achievement gap will have three years to learn material and acquire skills essential to the next level of knowledge. Our accelerated students can continue to be challenged to move ahead to even higher levels of achievement.

Goal Statement: It is the goal of Triangle Elementary School to provide a learning environment that challenges all students, regardless of ability, to reach their fullest potential by engaging in appropriate and relevant learning experiences at their particular levels of development. Continuous progress will result in lower retention rates, fewer discipline problems, and better academic achievement. Evaluation of this program will show evidence of its effectiveness through parent, teacher, and student surveys, standardized test data, and student products and progress noted by ongoing quarterly assessments.

The news media (*Washington Post* and *Potomac News*) along with other researchers in the field presented some taunting remarks at the beginning of my initiative. With my staff as a support team, I continued to show the need for program change. Critics fail to realize that many successful programs and concepts originate out of the need to address problems. Programs such as Reading Recovery, Success for All, differentiated learning, whole language, balanced literacy, guided reading, and magnet programs all originated from some sort of need. Somebody took the risk to try something different, and it worked.

The waiver to implement continuous progress for literacy achievement was unanimously approved by the school board but not without some skepticism from a couple of board members. Once the school board waiver was approved, I continued to stress to all stakeholders that this program was neither a quick fix nor the panacea for all of our school's problems. However, I felt that it was the best solution for our school's literacy achievement problems. Throughout implementation, my staff and I were able to acknowledge improvement in students' literacy achievement. Within two years, our school ranked in the top twenty-five of forty schools in achievement, which was a great improvement from the previous ranking at the bottom of the forty schools. The *Washington Post* and our local newspaper, the *Potomac News*, monitored our program throughout the first year and a half. The first news article from the *Post* was called "A New Take on an Old Problem," and the headline in June of that year was "A Measure of Their Success." Once it was known that our students were making achievement gains, media attention dissipated.

Carbo, Dunn, and Dunn write, "In effect, we have wasted a great deal of time, money, and human energy in pursuit of a mythical best approach to teaching children to read. There is no best way; there are many different approaches—some of which are effective with some children and ineffective with others. Each youngster learns differently from every other one and it is the match between how the learner learns and how the method teaches that determines who learns what and how much" (1991, 1).

Schools and school districts almost always focus on single literacy programs to address the needs and strengths of diverse school divisions. Most of these programs are very expensive and cut deep into school budgets. Many times the program cost causes few funds to be left for teacher training over a period of time. Without proper training, many of these high-cost programs fail to produce expected results. When this happens, individual schools with unique needs may not reap the benefits of these programs.

WHO SHOULD TRY THIS PROGRAM AND WHY?

I don't want to give the impression that my approach will benefit only slow learners or schools that have high percentages of economic deprivation, because that isn't the case. This approach will benefit all primary students and schools in any setting (urban, suburban, rural, etc.). The primary purpose of this approach is to improve literacy achievement for all students. School districts generally seek innovative literacy programs whose primary focus is on the average-learning students. Students who are struggling and above average students are given suggestions within the program or texts for remediation or challenge activities. There is little learning content that is intense for students who are above average or gifted. In addition, little consideration is given to the idea that there are students who may need to accelerate to an advanced curriculum in literacy skills.

For example, if in a traditional first-grade class there is a group of three or four students making As in all areas of literacy instruction, the teacher would be pleased, but I would look for more challenging work or consider the possibility that these students may need to go on to the second-grade literacy curriculum. As another example, in another school where I was an administrator (prior to Triangle Elementary School), first- and second-grade students were given standardized tests in October, and some of my first-grade students scored at the ninety-ninth percentile in literacy skills. Why should these students continue with literacy instruction at that grade level when they have already demonstrated mastery of skills that will be taught at that level? Why are students who demonstrate mastery of one grade-level curriculum before the school year ends not allowed to move on to the next grade-level curriculum? It is as if they are in a holding pattern until the school says it is time to move ahead. When I see primary students doing this well, I question whether they are being challenged to their full potential. Most of the time, these students are given what is considered challenging assignments at their grade level and are asked to assist or mentor other classmates who may be struggling. This certainly is not a good use of these students' talents. The continuous progress approach provides flexibility for these students to move past the grade-level block to another curriculum without the concern that educators have about moving students into another curriculum.

The concerns about moving students into another grade-level curriculum come from the question, What will the second-grade teacher teach? Grade levels can block primary students from reaching their full potential while frustrating students who are forced into a grade-level curriculum because of age rather than readiness. Many times, to justify providing challenging instruction for students who stand out from other classmates, the solution is to recommend them for the gifted program. We have many students who are identified as gifted and placed in gifted programs because their needs cannot be met in the regular classroom. While there are some students who are truly gifted in these classes, there are some who are not. What this has done is weaken the gifted label. Students can be high achievers but not necessary *gifted* in its truest sense. High schools are addressing this issue by offering advanced classes in various subject areas.

If we can start advanced instruction for students at the elementary school level, we will have more students ready for advanced courses by the time they reach high school. Continuous progress at the primary levels gives students the chance to advance to more difficult instruction as each student indicates readiness. Therefore, continuous progress is not just for the slow learner or struggling student; it is flexible to meet the needs of students at all performance levels.

Schools with high percentages of students not reading at or above grade level by third grade or eight years of age should seriously consider reorganizing primary classes for literacy achievement. This is an effective approach to closing literacy gaps for our primary students. They will become proficient readers and writers. If we allow students to fall behind during the early years of schooling, they will continue to fall behind throughout their school years. Eventually, students who struggle through primary grades become frustrated, exhibit discipline problems, or develop low self-esteem. Low self-esteem can have a negative impact on student performance. According to Purkey, "In an investigation of the relationship between children's perceptions of themselves and their world while in kindergarten and their subsequent achievement in reading in the first grade, Lamy (1965) found that these perceptions, obtained from inferences made by trained observers, gave as good a perception of later reading achievement as intelligence test scores. When I.Q. and self-evaluations were combined, the predictive power was even greater. In concluding her study, Lamy suggested that the perceptions of a child about himself and his world are not only related to, but may in fact be causal factors in, his subsequent reading achievement" (1970, 23).

Tomlinson shares an interesting quote from Howard Gardner (in Siegel & Shaughnessy, 1994): "The biggest mistake of past centuries in teaching has been to treat all children as if they were variants of the same individual, and thus to feel justified in teaching them the same subjects in the same ways" (Tomlinson, 1999, 9).

In summary, the continuous progress program does have a major impact in schools that have large percentages of underachievers struggling in literacy. Literacy achievement is experienced by all students, whether below average, average, above average, or gifted.

CHALLENGES TO FACE

It is common for change in any organization to bring challenges. Anytime you have change taking place, there are going to be barriers to address as you go through the processes of development and implementation. I knew that implementing this nontraditional program was not going to be easy. Continuous progress asks people involved to give up what has been long-time tradition. Also, it requires thinking outside the box. A major task is gaining support from teachers, students, parents, and the central office. Each group has its own reasons for not wanting to be involved in school reform. When school reform takes place with little or no input from the primary people responsible for making it work, the reform will be short-lived.

New programs and initiatives take time, training, and resources. As leaders, we must make sure that everyone involved willingly embraces the program and commits to a successful outcome. As a rule of thumb, the word "change" in any organization immediately sparks negative reactions and anxiety among individuals who are expected to be involved in the process. We can quickly soften emotional tension by foreseeing concerns and preparing answers and supporting data (quantitative and qualitative). Teachers are the primary people involved from beginning to end, and with this in mind, I wanted to be prepared to respond in a knowledgeable and professional way to any concerns and to help alleviate anxiety. In fact, teachers will determine the success or failure of this program. I put together a list of possible questions teachers might ask, along with the answers to those questions. These questions included the following:

Why should we change what we are doing?
How will this change improve student achievement?
What are we going to do differently?
Is training involved? How much and when?
Is there teacher support throughout the process?
Do we have the resources?
What resources do we need?
What specific results are expected?
What is the timeline for development and implementation?

Parents are important to the success of this program because without their support our students will not make the achievement gains we expect to come from the program. Parents will want answers to the same first three questions teachers will ask. Other questions they will probably pose include the following: Are there other options that will give us the same results? How will parents be involved? How informed will they be kept regarding their child's progress and the progress of the program? As with teachers, there will be parents who are completely adamant about not changing what is already in place. This is expected and is one of the major challenges to address. You have to find strategies to get as many people on the supportive side as possible.

Before meeting with teachers and parents, I shared my proposal idea with our school superintendent. He reacted favorably to the idea but was concerned about the multitude of tasks needed to get this type of school reform accepted by others involved, namely teachers, parents, the community, and the school board. Along with the associate superintendent for instruction, he wanted additional research on various components of the proposal, which I provided by our second meeting. By the second meeting, tentative approval to move forward with the proposal was granted by both superintendents with the understanding that I had to have support from my teachers and staff. The majority had to be supportive and committed to this nontraditional approach. One small advantage with my teachers and staff was that they all agreed after reviewing the data that some type of change had to take place.

Schlechty writes,

> For change to occur, five functions must be fulfilled. First, the nature of the change must be conceptualized. Second, people who are going to be called on to support the change must be solicited and, where possible and appropriate, incorporated into the change process. Third, feedback from those who were not involved in the initial conceptualization but who will be called on for support must be solicited and, where possible and appropriate, incorporated into the change process. Fourth, activity to implement change must begin, and people must be motivated to act in directions indicated by change. Fifth, a system of ongoing support and training must be provided for those who are asked to support the change. (1990, 97)

When talking with teachers about the type of behavioral changes that should take place if they were going to successfully go through a school reform, I emphasized the following points: first, we must develop a common vision and purposeful outcome; second, you must be flexible and open to change; third, you must be self-motivated; fourth, you must feel a sense of commitment to what is to be accomplished; fifth, you must be willing to go through training (professional development) and to try new techniques; sixth, we must strengthen collaboration among and between grade-level colleagues; and, finally, we must commit to working in a school environment as a team-oriented learning community.

According to Dufour and Eaker, "Change is a complex and formidable task that is certain to be accompanied by pain and conflict. Many argue that pain is an essential element for initiating change, that the familiar status quo is always preferable to change until the traditional way of doing things results in considerable discomfort to those in the organization" (1998, 50).

As noted by Dufour and Eaker (1998, 51), John Kotter (1996) identifies the eight most common mistakes in the change process. Here is a look at what we did to keep from making these mistakes.

1. Allowing too much complacency: Kotter contends that the biggest mistake people make when trying to change organizations is to plunge ahead without establishing enough sense of urgency. *Our sense of urgency was created by indentifying continuous low achievement data in literacy proficiency.*

2. Failing to create a sufficiently powerful guiding coalition: Individuals working alone, no matter how competent or charismatic they are, will never have everything that is needed to overcome the powerful forces of tradition and inertia. *As school administrator, I created a professional environment that strengthened teacher and staff collaboration and gained commitment from teachers to work in a team-oriented learning community prior to involvement in the change process.*

3. Underestimating the power of vision: Vision helps to direct, align, and inspire the actions of the members of an organization. *The first task we performed as a faculty was developing a shared vision statement we could all commit to.*

4. Undercommunicating the vision by a power of 10: Without credible communication, and a lot of it, change efforts are doomed to fail. *Ongoing professional development in conjunction with strong collaboration within and across teams was implemented.*

5. Permitting structural and cultural obstacles to block the change process: Organizations often fail to address obstacles that

block change. The organization must make every effort to remove the structural and cultural barriers that threaten to impede the implementation of that vision. *A list of possible obstacles we could face as a faculty was discussed and a plan to address each was developed as we showed our commitment as a unit joined together for a common cause.*

6. Failing to create short-term wins: Change initiatives risk losing momentum if there are no short-term goals to reach and celebrate. *Teachers and students experienced increases in student performance and self-motivation after the first semester of program implementation. Students' achievement continued to go upward as students continued to meet with success at their development levels. Teachers felt good about teaching, and students felt good about learning.*

7. Declaring victory too soon: There is a difference between celebrating a win and declaring victory. *It was two years before we actually declared victory, which was when our school was recognized by the governor as one of two schools that showed high improvement gains on the state's Standard of Learning (SOL) tests.*

8. Neglecting to anchor changes firmly in the culture: Change sticks only when it is firmly entrenched in the school or organization's culture, as part of "the way we do things around here." *For the first two to three years, we continued working hard to maintain solid components of our program and reevaluated on an annual basis what was working and what was not.*

As noted by Dufour and Eaker, Kotter continues, "These eight common mistakes represent potential minefields for those attempting to traverse the perilous path of transforming a school from its industrial traditions into a learning community" (1998, 53).

School reform will always be challenging, but a systematic approach to planning will not only alleviate the amount of stress and frustration but will also ensure that efforts are rewarded with successful results. Anything less will not be worth the effort.

LINKING LITERACY INSTRUCTION TO
CONTINUOUS PROGRESS

The principle behind continuous progress is developmental readiness, and every child progresses at his or her own level of growth. During the early nineties, when continuous progress was somewhat common as an alternative organizational school structure, it was not connected to a specific curriculum, and students were not grouped by performance in classrooms. Schools organized for continuous progress left groups the same in terms of heterogeneousness. Sometimes grade-level barriers were eliminated; however, teachers allowed students to work at their own pace within the heterogeneous class structure. The continuous progress concept dominated the instructional program. The learning environment was structured for student success within a diverse classroom because every student experiences success at his or her learning pace. Teachers maintained the mindset that every student in the class is not at the same level of development and experience, and because of this, each student will develop his or her knowledge base at different intervals. This meant that no student was looked down upon or thought of as a failure if he or she did not reach a certain knowledge level at the same time as his or her peers. Teachers provided a wide range of instructional activities for various learning levels to meet individual needs. Ongoing student evaluations were an intrinsic part of continuous progress.

As I began to search for some type of school improvement plan that would successfully address our need to increase literacy achievement, continuous progress was always on my mind as an ideal structure for the diverse performance levels throughout our primary grades. With primary retention rates so high due to students' not achieving expected standards in literacy achievement, we needed a structure that would not expose our primary students to school failure at such young ages. The principle behind continuous progress is what we needed to support our organizational structure in the primary grades. Continuous progress provides students the flexibility to progress at individual levels of performance.

Even though the premise of continuous progress will help with organizational structure, it is not enough to remove the stigma of grade-level failure because if you have first-grade students of different performance levels in a class and every child is given the opportunity to work at his or her own pace, how long will the slower-pace students remain at that level, and how far can the fast-pace students go? As this same first-grade class moves into a second-grade class, are some students considered low second, middle second, or high second because of their learning paces? With this as a concern, removal of grade-level designations seemed appropriate for the continuous progress structure. Without grade-level designations, primary students lose the stigma of failure because students are not forced into a curriculum because of grade level, nor do students have to remain in a curriculum that they may have already mastered simply because of grade level.

Given the research basis of a nongraded continuous progress structure, it seemed like a meaningful start to an educational reform that would address the lack of student success and achievement in the primary grades. Even though my focus for school reform was the primary grades, my ultimate goal was improving literacy achievement at all grade levels (K–5). The primary grades are where literacy development starts, and if students have difficulty at primary levels and nothing is done to address these difficulties, students' learning gaps get wider as they move up the ladder to upper grade levels.

In the primary grades, the instructional program revolves around literacy development. I use the term *literacy development* to mean reading, writing, and vocabulary development. More than 50 percent of my primary students showed such low achievement in these literacy areas that literacy became my primary focus for school reform. Math scores were considered low when compared to scores of other schools in the district, but there was a much higher percentage of failure in literacy.

Primary reading skills are the same no matter what basal reader a school district uses. The differences in content between basal readers are the scope and sequence of basic reading and language skills and the various techniques and strategies for the teaching of them. Therefore, infusing our primary reading and language skills into the nongraded continuous progress structure was not a major overhaul. A committee of primary teachers worked along with me to look at literacy skills from kindergarten to third grade. The skills were grouped for scope and sequence by structural analysis and comprehension. Then we chunked each section into a hierarchy of continuous student progress levels in the form of a continuum.

Some unique features of this organizational approach to instruction are the performance grouping of primary students on a hierarchy of continuous progress levels, frequent and ongoing literacy evaluations, and flexibility for student level movement during the school year. It took time to look at reading skills and make decisions about where each group should start on the continuum, and we reevaluated skill levels each year to make certain that student needs were met.

In essence, I implemented the continuous progress and nongraded concept with the primary focus on literacy development for student placement and instruction. All other subjects were addressed through interdisciplinary instruction within each level. This organizational structure is very successful in closing achievement gaps so that students can gain rapid knowledge in areas of need, and in this instance the area of greatest need was literacy.

CHAPTER 2

How Does This Program Differ from the Traditional School Program?

There are several distinct differences between our traditional elementary school program and a continuous progress program. The components I will show in comparison between the two programs are heterogeneous grouping versus performance grouping, grade-level classes versus nongraded classes, annual student promotion versus biannual student promotion, annual assessments versus quarterly assessments, and within-class ability grouping versus flexible grouping.

Traditional school programs in elementary schools tend to group students heterogeneously. There have been times when homogeneous grouping was tried, but it seemed to receive a negative connotation because it led to tracking. Heterogeneous grouping is the primary way elementary students are placed in classes. The continuous progress program allows the flexibility to group primary students by performance levels. In this instance, literacy performance levels are how students are grouped. You will read later in this chapter how our performance grouping dispels the concept of tracking.

Traditional school programs assign grade-level designations to age-appropriate classes; for example, six-year-olds are considered first-graders, seven-year-olds are considered second-graders, and eight-year-olds are considered third-graders. The continuous progress program does not assign grade designations to classes. Primary levels or classes are nongraded, meaning that we do not acknowledge all six-year-olds as first-graders or all seven-year-olds as second-graders. We acknowledge them as primary students in nongraded levels of instruction. Designated grade levels are acknowledged when students enter fourth and fifth grades.

Traditional school programs generally give annual standardized achievement tests to all students. Results are rarely used to identify students' individual strengths and needs because of the turnaround time in receiving scores. Many schools rely on this one annual standardized evaluation as a view of the whole child, which is invalid. For example, high-stakes testing resulting from the NCLB Act mandates that every state administer SOLs (Standards of Learning tests) to students in third and fifth grades at the elementary level. The results, thus far, are used to praise schools for high scores and "belittle" schools that do not achieve the standards as designated by state officials.

According to Wheelock, "The job of running a school, which encompasses tasks that are routine and those that are unpredictable, simply leaves little extra time for gathering and analyzing the data that can help schools move toward more potent practice. What's more, the data schools compiled long after the test's administration are passed on to the schools themselves only after they are reported in the local newspapers." Wheelock continues, "In many communities, published reports of student achievement defined by annual test score successes boost the price of real estate. In other communities, such data become the rationale for a steady disinvestment in public education. More recently, policymakers have moved to use selected data in high-stakes accountability schemes to 'reward' schools for test score improvements and to 'punish' those that do not post gains" (2002, xii).

The continuous progress program focuses on progression of student achievement. We identify individual strengths and needs of students rather than group strengths and needs. Every student's performance is evaluated on an individual basis, and instruction is provided according to individual needs. We waste instructional time by teaching students in areas that are mastered. Continuous progress mandates that students should not spend time on what they have already mastered nor move on to more difficult instruction for which they have no background knowledge to achieve success. With this philosophical belief, we have to assess student achievement more frequently than once a year. At Triangle Elementary School, we chose to assess and analyze student achievement quarterly and continue to use the annual standardized achievement test in addition to SOLs with students in grades other than third and fifth.

Traditional schools promote students to other grade levels once a year. This once-a-year occurrence is in June. Students are locked into one grade level of instruction for nine months regardless of their actual level of performance. For example, suppose a student who is in second grade shows performance below grade level. Will instruction be adapted to get this student's performance up to grade-level expectations? On the other end, suppose a student in second grade performs above this grade level. Will instruction be adapted to keep this student challenged? Students on either end of the spectrum have to remain for nine months in an instructional environment that is not directly addressing their performance needs.

Continuous progress is flexible in movement or promotion of students. Because students are not locked into designated grade levels, they can move to whatever performance level will meet their individual needs twice within a nine-month school year. Quarterly student assessments help teachers identify students who show mastery of current instruction and need another challenge. They also help teachers identify students who may need additional time to master current levels of instruction. We have the flexibility to move or promote students in January and in June. We do not have to wait until the end of a school year to move students to appropriate instructional levels.

Traditional schools assign elementary students to classes based on a heterogeneous grouping plan. Because students are heterogeneously grouped, performance levels in these classes are diverse and therefore require teachers to regroup students into homogeneous literacy instruction groups within their classrooms or to teach the whole class of students as if they are all at the same level of performance. This is their way of providing materials and resources that will address unique needs and abilities within traditional classrooms. The problem here is having too many groups; instruction takes monumental planning time, and the major part of the day is spent rotating small literacy groups. Students generally remain in their small group the entire school year. There is very little reshuffling of these skill groups. Students are viewed as a group and move according to their group.

Continuous progress assigns primary students to performance levels based on assessments of entrance-level literacy skills. Students are assigned to levels according to specific skill needs. Teachers analyze student data and provide instruction that addresses individual needs and thereby closes the achievement gap in those identified areas. Because students are in levels with similar achievement gaps in literacy skills, teachers are able to plan effectively for skill instruction. Flexible grouping allows teachers to focus on specific skills, and as students show mastery of certain skills, they can move among skill groups. Students can change skill groups weekly or bimonthly based on their performance.

Anderson and Pavan write,

> The research studies on nongraded, multigraded, and ungraded grouping support the viability of this organizational concept. In most cases, students in schools organized in one of the above styles do as well as or better than students in traditional self-contained classes in terms of both academic achievement and mental health measures. This is in spite of the fact that the instruments used to measure achievement and mental health often are standardized on students in traditionally structured schools.
>
> The true philosophy of nongradedness is the belief that individuals are unique and need different treatments to reach their maximum growth potential. Some nongraded programs reflect this belief whereas others have demonstrated a limited acceptance of this belief by allowing students to set only their own pace with materials, methods, and goals predetermined. (1993, 43)

Two of the components above caused a bit of controversy at my school. Performance grouping and the concept of nongraded classes (removal of grade-level designations) initially seemed to alarm parents, other educators, and some researchers in this field. This was no surprise to me or my staff because the mention of these words without contextual understanding can narrow one's perception. Both components have always led to controversy in the past and will continue to do so. The parent reaction was no surprise to me because it is understandable for parents to want to be assured that their children are getting the best education possible, and the traditional school structure was all they knew and felt comfortable with. Some parents and educators were willing to remain open to our reform movement, but many started out against it.

The news media added to the level of discomfort as they wrote some taunting remarks about our program through interviews with other educational researchers. According to O'Hanlon, one interview comment that was positive came from June Million, spokeswoman for the National Association of Elementary School Principals, who stated, "Triangle's approach seems to make sense. It sounds like good education to me. It sounds like the school is meeting the needs of the individual child, which is the idea" (1997, 6).

O'Hanlon interviewed Robert Slavin, founder of Success for All, who gave this comment: "What is different about this idea is that they are going to have students grouped all day according to their reading performance. I don't know of anybody doing that" (O'Hanlon, 1997, 6). O'Hanlon also interviewed Samuel Stringfield, principal research scientist at the Johns Hopkins Center for the Social Organization of Schools, who stated, "Programs that group children by their ability don't seem to have much effect on academic performance. It hasn't had strong impact on student achievement, either pro or con, in most programs. Such programs have been criticized for not being aggressive enough in bringing weak students up to grade level. People get worried that you are going to have concentrations of less advantaged kids . . . in those bottom classes and that you are going to have these nice little at-grade and above-level girls in the top classes" (O'Hanlon, 1997, 6).

While there may be some merit to these comments, there is more to the continuous progress approach than ability grouping. Grouping students for instruction has always been in debate. Heterogeneous versus homogeneous: is one better than the other? My answer is that it depends on the purpose. Many confused our performance grouping with ability grouping, which much research says is harmful and an ineffective method for instructing students. In fact, I continued to stress that we were grouping by performance, not by ability. What is the difference? When you speak of ability grouping, you are saying that all students within a group have the same IQ (intelligence quotient). While this type of grouping might have been used years ago, it is not what happens in performance grouping. Performance grouping means placing students with the same skill needs and strengths together. For example, the fact that a group of students are weak in the same literacy skill area does not mean that every student in that group has the same IQ. Students' IQs are not a part of our placement decisions. Our goal as administrators and teachers is to provide the best literacy-rich learning environment that will enable our students to reach their maximum potential.

Kulik writes, "Effects of grouping programs depend on their features. Some grouping programs have little or no effect on students; other programs have moderate effects; and still other programs have large effects. The key distinction is among (a) programs in which ability groups follow the same curriculum, (b) programs in which all groups follow curricula adjusted to their ability, and (c) programs that make curricular and other adjustments for special needs and high talented learners" (1993).

The continuous progress approach eliminates the problem of students' becoming stagnated and eliminates the practice of forcing students into things they are not developmentally ready to do. Removal of grade-level designations in primary school is not a problem or concern of the students; it is a major concern for parents and certain educators.

According to Gaustad,

Graded education assumes that students who are the same age are basically the same level of cognitive development, can be taught in the same way, and will progress at the same rate. Intellectual development is assumed to be the goal, and the division of curriculum into discrete skills and subjects to be the most effective organization. Research has discredited all these assumptions. Young children actually vary in their rates of intellectual development just as they do in physical development. They often progress at different rates in different areas of achievement and may alternately spurt ahead and hit plateaus rather than moving at a steady pace. (1992b, 3)

In summary, the continuous progress approach was put in place to increase literacy proficiency of primary students. Our primary goal was to have all students reading at or above grade level by third grade. In order to get maximum results from intense individualized literacy instruction, a comprehensive assessment plan was put in place to identify level placement for students. Traditional schools place students according to age and grade level. Assessments are not used to place students. Because our approach was nongraded, students were given the flexibility to move twice a year to more difficult levels of literacy instruction.

Traditional school programs keep students at one grade level for the entire school year whether they need that curriculum or not. Imposed grade-level designations block student movement once mastery is achieved. Where a student begins literacy instruction should be determined by skill needs and strengths, but age determines where students begin literacy instruction in traditional settings. In traditional school programs, retention is the primary option when students do not perform well in the curriculum for their assigned grade level. In our approach, students are not retained in the truest sense of the word. Students progress as gaps close in their learning process. Standardized evaluations at the end of the year are used to evaluate student achievement in most traditional programs. In the continuous progress program, students are involved in quarterly evaluations to assess their literacy skills.

PERFORMANCE GROUPING VERSUS TRACKING

How schools group students for instruction is always controversial in discussion and decision making. There are pros and cons for both homogeneous and heterogeneous groups. However, heterogeneous grouping is utilized by most school divisions. One primary reason is that, according to research, students are able to learn from each other, and if you have struggling students grouped with high achievers, the struggling students are going to learn from other students in class; hence, high achievers are role models for struggling students.

Homogeneous grouping is associated with the idea of tracking. The word *tracking* causes eyebrows to rise and discussion to shut down immediately. According to Goodlad, "Tracking became widely practiced by educators as a device for endeavoring to reduce the range of differences in class and therefore the difficulty and complexity of the teaching task. The practice has been reinforced from outside the school by those who believe that able students are held back by slower ones when all work together in the same class" (1984, 151).

Tracking has been associated with minority and low socioeconomic groups. The mindset is often that students in low-track classes are minorities who come from deprived homes and therefore their instruction has to be watered down for lack of understanding. With low teacher expectations, they can learn only so much, and the pace has to be very slow, whereas the mindset for high-track classes is that students who come from privileged homes are more knowledgeable and can learn at a faster pace. Students were known to remain in the same track from elementary through high school, the reason for this stemming from the fact that once you are labeled as slow, you will always be just that.

When I presented the idea of performance grouping according to specific skill needs, the first reaction from some seasoned educators and others was that I was talking about tracking. This idea will be dispelled as you learn more about performance grouping as compared to tracking.

In traditional primary classrooms where students are heterogeneously grouped, teachers always develop homogeneous subgroups for reading and language instruction. Teachers find frustration in trying to meet the needs of individual students within the heterogeneous classroom because of the range of performance levels. There could be five or six literacy performance levels in one classroom. And what discipline do primary teachers spend most of the school day teaching? Literacy. What has happened over the last five to ten years, which is probably the root cause of so many students' deficiencies in literacy, is that diverse levels of performance have led to some primary teachers instructing whole-class groups in literacy and no longer trying subgrouping to meet diverse needs and development levels. This means everyone in the class is considered to be at the same level of reading performance. Therefore, in a class of twenty-two students, every student is on the same page doing the same assignment regardless of where their performance actually is.

Another way I have observed teachers teaching reading with whole-class groups is by dividing students into smaller groups but using the same text and teaching materials and keeping everyone on the same page. Again, the teacher is making the assumption that every student is at the same level of performance. Some of today's teachers are not going to put the extra effort into planning for several reading groups, and therefore they make the decision to teach everyone the same way. This type of whole-group instruction in literacy increases the likelihood that many students are not proficient readers by third grade.

According to Au, Carroll, and Scheu, "In Vygotsky's Zone of Proximal Development, Vygotsky states that the zone represents the 'difference between the child's actual level of development and the level of performance that he achieves in collaboration with the adult'" (1997, 15). Au, Carroll, and Scheu provide this example: "A kindergarten child who can read simple, predictable books probably will not benefit from prolonged instruction in reading similar books. Beyond the zone, the child will not benefit either because the level of performance demanded is too difficult. For example, the same kindergarten child probably will not benefit from instruction in reading a chapter book with few pictures, because these books are far too difficult. To help a child learn, the teacher must engage him in a performance of just the right degree of difficulty" (1997, 15).

Listed below are three concerns about performance grouping. These concerns are legitimately noted because if educators are not careful in how and why specific grouping arrangements occur, our students can be victims as the result. Fountas and Pinnell (1996, 97) report the following concerns, according to research by a committee of the Massachusetts Reading Association:

1. Assigning students to self-contained classes or tracks within classes according to achievement or ability does not enhance achievement. Once a child is assigned to a low group, the chances of moving to a higher group are very low.
2. Students in high and low ability groups receive different instruction. For example, children in low ability groups receive slow, watered-down instruction, while students in higher ability groups receive challenging, fast-paced instruction.
3. Students' self-confidence and self-esteem are damaged by their assignment to low groups.

The continuous progress approach addresses the first concern because every teacher's instructional goal in the program is to have as many students as possible move out of their classes by midyear (second semester). Therefore, students have the opportunity to progress to instructional levels that are more difficult. When teachers can instruct students with similar skill needs and strengths, they can plan more effectively for intense, solid literacy instruction. More quality time is spent teaching smaller groups because performance grouping doesn't mean the teacher will instruct all students at that level as a whole group. The teacher is expected to have subgroups within each performance group. This truly allows teachers to meet individual needs because the performance range is narrow enough to allow two small subgroups, compared to the five to six in traditional classes with wider performance ranges.

Hollifield shares Slavin's view on how grouping affects student achievement in a nongraded plan. "This plan includes a variety of related grouping plans that place students in flexible groups according to performance rather than age. Thus, grade-level designations are eliminated. The curriculum for each subject is divided into levels through which students progress at their own rates. Well-controlled studies conducted in regular schools generally support the use of comprehensive nongraded plans" (1987, 1).

Concern number two is addressed by teacher expectations. As a professional goal, every teacher in the program is expected to model high expectations for all students no matter what levels they perform at. Professional development training provides teaching strategies and techniques for literacy instruction. Teachers at all levels receive the same training on strategies and techniques. For example, we have professional development training on vocabulary development. Teachers at all levels are expected to implement the strategies presented. Teachers implement the strategies and techniques at their students' vocabulary level with the understanding that the goal is to build upon what they already know to build a more extensive vocabulary. Therefore, the instruction is not watered down because no matter what level, the same teaching strategies are implemented by all teachers.

The third concern addresses students' self-esteem. According to Hollifield, "One of the main arguments against ability grouping is that the practice creates classes or groups of low achievers who are deprived of the example and stimulation provided by high achievers. Labeling students according to ability and assigning them to low-achievement groups may also communicate self-fulfilling low expectations. Further, groups with low performance often received a lower quality of instruction than other groups" (1987, 1). However, the concern regarding students' self-esteem is questionable because students feel good about themselves when they experience success. This is human nature. Therefore, literacy levels on the continuum give students the chance to experience immediate success because of placement at their developmental level of performance. After one semester, we saw not only improvement in literacy achievement but also improvement in students' self-esteem and self-motivation. In fact, our discipline problems drastically declined, and we experienced an increase in school attendance. Parents saw positive changes in their children's attitude toward school.

Purkey writes, "Success and failure in school significantly influence the ways in which students view themselves. Students who experience repeated success in school are likely to develop positive feelings about their abilities, while those who encounter failure tend to develop negative views of them. In the light of influence of self-concept on academic achievement, it would seem like a good idea for schools to follow the precept I saw printed on an automobile drag-strip racing program: 'Every effort is made to insure that each entry has a reasonable chance of victory'" (1970, 26). The process in place to avoid harming our students by ability grouping is the progressive approach to moving students up to more difficult skills as they show mastery and readiness.

LEVEL PROGRESSION

The flexibility of the continuum provides students the opportunity to move upward as they show readiness to enter another group. Students move along the continuum in January and June. I will discuss movement within levels 1 to 5 as an example of how movement occurs. Kindergarten students are not considered for movement until second semester (January). For example, in January a kindergarten teacher has four students who are well on their way in reading development. In fact, they are able to read books at reading level 1.5 and above. These students can be recommended for placement in level 1 or level 2. By January, students in level 1 (who entered level 1 in September) are now at reading level 1.0 or 1.3. Therefore, the kindergarten students can enter this level. In the meantime, there are students in level 1 who progress to level 3 in January. Out of fifteen students at level 1 in September, nine are recommended for movement because mastery was achieved. Four kindergarten students move into level 1, and nine students move out of level 1 in January. The students remaining at level 1 need more time to accomplish mastery of all the skills. The level 1 teacher will not go back to any part of his or her instruction because the four kindergarten-age students who entered the level can pick up where the instruction is at that point and move ahead. The teacher never drops back; instruction continues to move ahead in skill development.

You may ask whether these kindergarten students will move from level 1 to 6a in June. No, they will most likely progress to level 4 (reading level 1.4 to 1.5) or level 5 (reading level 1.6 to 1.9) depending on individual performance data. Students do not move into levels by groups but by individual needs. The continuum in figure 1.1 shows that there are four literacy skill levels these students would skip if they went to level 6a, which is second-team curriculum. As another example, in September there are twenty students in level 5. By midyear, nine of these students demonstrate complete mastery of literacy skills at this level. The teacher recommends them for movement to team two. Team two has four levels (6a, 6b, 7a, 7b). The first level, 6a, is equivalent in September to reading level 2.0. Student placement is based on individual strengths and data; therefore, a teacher can recommend students for any of the four levels. Two may go into level 6a, three may go into 6b, and so forth. Placement decisions are based on where each student will experience the maximum success and continue moving ahead.

According to Grossen (1996),

The studies of elementary school grouping alternatives have more complete descriptions of the instruction than the secondary studies of grouping. After using 'best evidence synthesis' to seek out patterns of positive and negative effects in 43 studies comparing school grouping arrangements, Slavin was able to conclude: Taken together, the evidence points to a conclusion that for ability grouping to be effective at the elementary level, it must create true homogeneity on the specific skill being taught and instruction must be closely tailored to students' level of performance." (1996, 4)

USING PERFORMANCE DATA TO CLOSE LITERACY ACHIEVEMENT GAPS

One major component of the continuous progress program is the use of data to close literacy gaps. I use the term *performance data* because the assessments we administer give us specific information about students' performance levels, in this case performance in literacy (reading, writing, and vocabulary development). In order to achieve our goals by implementing a continuous progress approach to increase literacy achievement, there has to be frequent monitoring of student achievement. I developed an assessment/accountability plan whereby teachers would assess students' literacy skills on at least a quarterly basis. Also, in this plan teachers have to analyze the results and use this information to plan and adjust their instruction. This data analysis helps teachers make instructional decisions about individual students' needs and strengths.

Administering one standardized test at the end of a school year cannot provide the data needed to make instructional decisions throughout the school year. One major problem with relying on a single standardized test is the fact that districts do not get results until close to the end of the school year and sometimes in the later part of summer. By this time, students have moved on, and so have teachers. When this happens, individual student results are put in students' school files and sent to the next year's teacher, who probably will not look at the results.

The primary reason for our school reform plan was to close students' literacy achievement gaps throughout our school (K–5). We selected assessment measures that teachers could analyze and use to direct their instruction. We did not want students to repeat or receive instruction in literacy areas that they had already mastered nor did we want to overlook literacy areas that were yet not mastered.

Our program required frequent monitoring of student performance. Through frequent monitoring, teachers can make effective decisions about improving student performance and student placement. If teachers did less monitoring and analyzing of performance data, the school reform plan would not be viable. According to Schmoker, "Ron Edmonds writes, 'The days are long gone when an educator's best judgment constitutes sufficient proof of learning outcomes.' One of the principles of effective schools that he fathered is that successful schools 'frequently monitor progress'" (1996, 32). We identified three literacy performance measures that primary teachers would administer quarterly (September, January, and June). As I list each assessment below, I give its function as it relates to measuring student achievement in literacy skills.

A *miscue analysis* is administered quarterly to primary students on an individual basis. The level teacher, not the reading specialist, is required to administer this assessment. My rationale for this is that the level teacher is responsible for achieving results and he or she needs to know specific information regarding skill deficiencies. Listening to each student read a passage gives teachers better insight as to how to instruct individual students.

We also use this assessment with new students. The reading teacher/specialist administers a miscue analysis to all incoming new students before placing them on the continuum. When a new student enrolls, we schedule a time to administer a miscue analysis and obtain a writing sample. Results from both assessments are analyzed. Once results are analyzed, I share them with parents and make a recommendation for placement on our continuum based on the child's individual needs and strengths.

I feel strongly about the use of miscue analysis at the primary level because it analyzes a student's precise reading behaviors.

Teachers administer miscue analysis by providing the student with a reading passage according to age and expected grade level to read without assistance (this is key: no coaching). The teacher listens, observes, and records how the child is reading. The focus is on fluency, word skipping, unknown words, self-corrections, use of punctuation cues, and so forth in an effort to identify the areas the student needs to work on to improve reading skills and comprehension. If a student reads the first passage successfully, the teacher continues to administer the next higher level passage until the student scores less than 90 percent accuracy in independent reading of a passage. Any score below 90 is considered too difficult a passage for the student to read without assistance. When students score between 90 and 94 percent, the passage is considered at the appropriate instructional level, which is considered the starting level for instruction. Ninety-five percent or above is too easy. For example, if a second-grade student scores 95 or above on a reading 2.1 (considered second grade, first month) he or she needs a higher level reading passage because this is too easy. If a student experiences difficulty reading the first passage, the teacher drops back until the student gets a score of 90 percent.

We instituted a *writing assessment* beginning in kindergarten. Writing, to me, is another means to reading. Schools think of writing instruction as teaching students how to form letters in print and manuscript. We continue to teach letter formation at the primary levels, but we also teach writing as a process for communication. Our writing instruction serves three purposes. The first is to increase students' thinking and reading skills, the second is to increase vocabulary, and the third is to develop at an early stage skills needed for the state's fourth-grade writing test. Writing was also an area where my students scored very low on the state's fourth-grade evaluations.

To wait until students reach fourth grade to introduce them to writing does not give them enough experience or preparation, especially for students who are low achievers. As a staff, we looked at the writing domains targeted by the state for evaluation. A checklist of targeted writing domains was developed and organized into individual scoring charts for teachers to use as an evaluation of students' progress in each domain. Primary and intermediate teachers provided instruction in each of these areas. At the end of each quarter, as with the reading assessment, students are given a prompt or topic to write about without assistance. Topics are assigned according to teams. For example, every student on team one writes about the same topic. Teachers score students' writing paragraphs, evaluating their writing in five areas: composing (one consistent message, clear purpose, following a plan for writing, fully developed main idea, story sequence), usage (grammar, word meaning, and agreement), style (creativity, point of view), sentence formation (use of mature and complete sentences), and mechanics (capitalization, punctuation, and spelling).

We use a numerical scoring system from 0 to 4. A score of 0 indicates not scorable, 1 indicates little or no control, 2 indicates inconsistent control, 3 indicates reasonable control, and 4 indicates consistent control. The goal is to obtain a score of 4 in all areas by the third quarter (end of school year). Teachers provide written comments to support their numerical scores. Teachers also know in which specific areas individual students need additional instruction. This was very helpful for teachers in directing their writing instruction. The entire process proved to be instrumental in increasing students' literacy achievement in the areas of reading, writing, vocabulary, and language development.

We administer the *Gates-MacGinitie* assessment in grades four and five. Some third-team students may also be given this assessment if they test out of miscue levels. Even though restructuring was done in the primary grades, we felt the need to institute quarterly literacy assessments in the intermediate grades. The Gates-MacGinitie assessment was chosen as it provided teachers with a measure of students' achievement in vocabulary knowledge, vocabulary usage, and reading comprehension. Teachers are able to identify specific areas of comprehension and need and therefore either provide direct instruction in those areas for students who need it or know what skills to maintain. For example, the results of this assessment identify comprehension areas such as main idea, cause and effect, drawing conclusions, and predicting outcomes. This test is administered to each class as a whole, not individually as with miscue analysis for primary students.

The *Stanford Achievement Test* is a standardized test we administer schoolwide on an annual basis. Students are tested only in reading, language, spelling, and math. I wanted another evaluation measure that would validate the results of our quarterly assessments. We found that Stanford results were very close to students' results on their quarterly assessments. In fact, there were no surprises when teachers compared results of both measurements.

The above assessments provided teachers with much success in identifying individual students' literacy gaps, and by doing so, teachers were able to direct their instruction to those needed areas to close gaps that impeded student achievement. Incorporating these quarterly assessments also strengthened students' test-taking skills. I always believed many students were unfairly judged by standardized test results because they lacked test-taking skills. I therefore worked with teachers to develop a program for teaching test-taking skills to our students. Putting their knowledge into practice through quarterly assessments helped students develop these skills. Students' improved test-taking skills helped increase student performance on state testing such as SOLs.

As Schmoker (1996) points out in Rosenholtz's (1991) comment, "School success depends upon how effectively we select, define, and measure progress and how well we adjust effort toward goals. School goals tell teachers what should be emphasized instructionally and define for schools and teachers how they should gauge their performance success" (1996, 20).

Lortie writes, "The monitoring of student progress stands at the heart of instruction" (1975, 41).

RETHINKING RETENTION

According to Roderick (1995), "Grade retention rates and, as a result, the proportion of students overage for grade by the time they reach high school have risen nearly 40 percent over the past decades. Many teachers believe that retention, particularly in the early grades, is an effective strategy to remediate poor school performance and may reduce the likelihood of later school failure. Research on grade retention, however, concludes that repeating a grade provides few remediation benefits and may, in the long run, place students at higher risk of dropping out of school" (1995, 1). In 2006, Oprah Winfrey had a show on school crisis. On this show, a guest named Ms. Schwartz who developed a school within a jail in Los Angeles stated that 75 percent of their inmates were high school dropouts with third- to seventh-grade reading levels.

The continuous progress program does not acknowledge retention in its truest sense. In traditional school programs, most students who are retained are held back in first and second grades. Poor literacy development is the primary reason for student retention during the first three years of school. The continuous progress approach eliminates retention and the negativity attached to it. Roderick writes, "Results of studies investigating the effects of retention on academic performance generally indicate that retention as a means of remediation does not work. At best, it leaves students who were already lagging behind their peers even further behind" (1995, 4).

With the removal of strict grade-level designations, and with administering quarterly literacy assessments, teachers are able to more quickly identify the skill areas in which students need more assistance and can provide the additional instruction before students get to the point where catching up is more difficult for them. Performance groupings allow teachers the flexibility to move students who are ready to move up and to continue intense instruction for students who need that extra time. In the continuous progress program, a student can remain at one performance level for the entire school year if needed, which is the same as a student remaining in the same classroom all year. With all the individualization and intensity of instruction, if a student fails to make the progress expected by the end of the year, this is a red flag that we may need to consider recommending the student for special services (a special education program). This does not mean an automatic decision for placement in these services, but we take students through a thorough evaluation process for a closer look.

As a result, students' learning problems do not go unidentified until they reach third or fourth grade. This happens quite often in traditional programs, and by that time the learning problem has magnified. According to our program guidelines, the maximum time a student can remain at one performance level is one year and one semester; however, if a student continues to show very slow development by the end of one year at a performance level, it is a red flag for further attention. Students who remain at one performance level for the entire school year do not repeat instruction because, as stated earlier, the teacher continues to move instruction forward and must find other means or techniques for increasing learning.

In traditional school programs, many struggling students are recommended for retention, and some are actually retained, while others may be promoted and continue to struggle. One advantage of continuous progress is that students can progress without frustration, and therefore the students themselves become self-motivated to accomplish what is needed to be successful.

WHAT HAPPENS WHEN STUDENTS TRANSFER?

I wasn't sure whether to consider this a challenge or just a difference between the traditional school program and the continuous progress approach. Student transfer was not a true challenge for us; however, it presented us with many questions from receiving schools.

When I started compiling a list of questions and concerns I had to address when presenting this unique program for waiver approval, the question of what happens when students transfer never entered the equation. My focus was on developing the program and ensuring success in terms of student achievement. In fact, during the waiver process the school board and superintendent never raised this concern. As I look back, this question should have had an answer, not just for our school but for all other schools within the county.

Students in my school were fairly transitory, as were students in other schools within our district. Some schools in our district rarely had student turnover, but most of those schools were in residential areas. My school area accommodated five or six housing developments, three battered women's shelters, and residential areas. It was evident that such a school would have students frequently coming in, going out, and returning again.

The concern expressed by other school administrators was appropriate student placement in their building since we did not acknowledge grade levels. It has been my experience that a school completes a transfer form when a student moves to another school within the district. The form asks for the child's current grade level so that the receiving school will place the student in the same grade level as in the previous school. We modified our student transfer form to list performance levels in reading and math. For example, a seven-year-old student is considered a second grader according to age. His or her performance placement is in level 4, which is on the first team. A level 4 is equivalent to a reading level of 1.5, which is below grade-level expectation. The question for the receiving school becomes, does this student go into a traditional second-grade classroom or first grade?

As a staff, we made the decision to not make recommendations for receiving schools unless students were a year or two below expected performance. We sent miscue analysis results, vocabulary tests, writing assessments, and math evaluations. Receiving schools could use this data as we did to make the appropriate decision for placement together with the parent.

My colleagues complained and did not care for making these types of decisions. Therefore, I was not the most popular administrator among some of my colleagues, but I still had several who valued what we were doing to address the unique and immediate needs at my school site. In fact, one of the area superintendents (not my immediate supervisor) discussed with me the possibility of requesting that our school become a specialty (magnet) school. If this happened, students would not have to transfer out if they moved; they could remain at our school until completion of the continuous progress program and receive bus transportation. She indicated that she could see a difference in my students' self-esteem and motivation for learning. They felt successful and were making progress in closing achievement gaps. To have students transfer to another school would probably be devastating to their self-esteem and learning if they found themselves in learning situations they were not yet able to handle. The suggestion, for whatever reasons, did not fit into instructional plans overseen by our assistant superintendent for instruction. Nevertheless, our program moved forward with continued success. We continued with the same transfer process, but if I had it to do over again, I would present this program as a specialty school.

CHAPTER 3

Reorganizing for Continuous Progress

LEADERSHIP AND SUPPORT

This chapter examines steps that must be taken to reorganize primary grades into a continuous progress program and looks at how continuous progress is addressed by looping at intermediate grades. I developed a systematic approach to this change process. There are five major steps to developing and implementing this type of school reform. Any school administrator must know and understand that when school reform takes place at your school site, there is going to be conflict and pain, and as school leaders, we should be seen as the risk taker at the forefront for leadership and support. When I led my school through the reform process, I would not have achieved success without going through several stages in a systematic manner. The stages are as follows:

Leadership and support—Leadership, in this instance, is the school principal. Someone has to take the lead in developing plans, researching, and being the liaison for all people involved throughout the process. You will read about the principal's role as well as the roles of teachers, parents, and central office personnel.

Establishment of an effective learning culture—This is an integral part of any reform movement. If a change for improvement is to come about, then the culture of the school must change as well. Cultural changes are generally imparted through the organization's vision and goals. Encouraging collaboration strengthens a school's culture. Parent involvement is part of this stage because parents are stakeholders in the learning community.

Professional development—This area needs much attention and should always be included in reforms for improvement. Many reforms do not successfully achieve their goals because they lack a strong training component. If you are looking to improve in certain areas, people involved in those areas must be trained so that they can make the necessary changes.

Evaluation of program components—You must address areas that are going to be newly developed or changed. What requires improvement, and what are we putting in place of what we have?

Steps to school reform—Go back over the process and evaluate how effective each part of the process was in achieving the expected outcome. Look at how each part could have been done better.

According to Dufour and Eaker (1998), "Change is a complex and formidable task that is certain to be accompanied by pain and conflict. Many argue that pain is an essential element for initiating change, that the familiar status quo is always preferable to change until the traditional way of doing things results in considerable discomfort to those in the organization. As Michael Fullan (1993) emphasized, 'Conflict is essential to any successful change effort'" (1998, 50).

Unless we can get teachers and staff to see the need for change and be willing to support it, change will not happen. At my school, I knew we would experience conflict because the proposed change was nontraditional even though the concept was not new. Educators have a long history of doing more of the same; therefore, to ask people to think in a direction that is not the norm causes them to be reluctant and present barriers to change.

According to Schlechty,

For change to occur, five functions must be fulfilled. First, the nature of the change must be conceptualized. Second, people who are going to be called on to support the change but who were not involved in the conception process must be made aware of the change. Third, feedback from those who were not involved in the initial conceptualization but who will be called on for support must be solicited and, where possible and appropriate, incorporated into the change process. Fourth, activity to implement the change must begin, and people must be motivated to act in directions indicated by change. Fifth, a system of ongoing support and training must be provided for those who are being asked to support the change. (1990, 97–98)

The Principal's Role

A principal (school administrator) is viewed as an effective leader when students demonstrate outstanding achievement, and when students perform poorly, the principal is viewed as an ineffective leader. Principals should be cognizant of their leadership style and always work toward maintaining a professional, collaborative environment in their school setting. The principal sets the climate and culture for learning in a building.

McEwan (2003) cites a report by Arthur Andersen LLP (1997) that states, "The key factor to the individual school's success is the building principal, who sets the tone as the school's educational leader, enforces the positive, and convinces the students, parents and teachers that all children can learn and improve academically. Our overall assessment is that the school principal has the greatest single impact on student performance. As a result we believe that increased attention and funding needs to be directed towards programs that attract, evaluate, train, and retain the best principals" (2003, 2).

The principal must take the lead not only in management of a school but also in school reform and improvement. Principals who do not see a need for improvement or are not willing to take risks will not see growth or improvement. Also, a principal cannot bring about change without the commitment of the individuals directly involved in the implementation. As Dufour and Eaker state, "A school improvement effort grounded in disdain or disregard for the professional staff is doomed to failure. It should be self-evident that the real key to improvement of any school is a commitment to the nurturing and professional development of its practitioners because in reality they are the school" (1992, 5).

I began involving my teachers and staff in realizing the need for change when I shared our students' achievement data. The data went back three years. They could see patterns of low achievement and sense, as I had hoped, that unless we looked at the way we were instructing our students, we would continue to receive the same results. Our school had the lowest student achievement scores of forty elementary schools in our district at that time. Teachers who worked hard were frustrated and turned off at continuing to put forth so much effort for so few results. Our percentage of students qualifying for free and reduced lunch was high, school attendance was low, and discipline was a schoolwide concern. In fact, we were one of two elementary schools with a behavioral specialist on staff.

My first task as the new principal of this school was to review current and previous achievement data. At that time, the Iowa Test of Basic Skills was the district assessment for grades two and four. According to the results for reading, 40.3 percent of our second-grade students scored in the bottom quartile, and 13 percent scored at the top. In fourth grade, 34.6 percent scored in the bottom quartile, and 7 percent scored at the top. Students were continually promoted to the next grade level with little or no mastery of skills from the previous grade level. This caused more frustration for the teachers who received students so far behind what they were expected to accomplish. There was little time built into the instructional day for remediation; therefore, teachers struggled with students who were struggling.

Teachers agreed that change in the instructional program was needed. As to what type of change, no one was sure. To get teachers to toss around ideas, I asked them to think backward for a moment. I asked them to list what they did not want to continue seeing in their school. They listed the following: first, a high percentage of literacy-deficient students; second, wide ranges of performance levels in classrooms; third, the need to drop back to teach literacy skills from previous grade levels; fourth, the many discipline problems that interrupted instruction; and fifth, poor attendance of students already behind.

After listing what they did not want to have continue at their school, they listed what would need to happen to increase student achievement. First, they wanted an increase in literacy achievement among all students; second, they wanted a policy that would not allow literacy-deficient students to be automatically promoted; and third, intermediate teachers (fourth and fifth grade) wanted to teach their curriculum effectively in other core subjects, which they found difficult because so many students were struggling with reading and comprehending the texts. Many modifications would have to be made to get the core subjects across to those students.

Fourth grade is where instruction begins to focus more on the core subjects of social studies, science, health, and mathematics. Students engage in higher levels of thinking such as application, synthesizing, and evaluation. As I monitored instruction and student learning, I found little evidence that students were utilizing these higher-level thinking skills and their core subject curriculums as expected. The concern seemed to lie in the fact that students in fourth and fifth grades were still in need of literacy skills that they should have mastered in the primary grades. That is why I felt the change must take place before students get into the intermediate grades.

After sharing achievement data and discussing what we needed to do to get to where we wanted to be, the teachers and I started sharing possible ideas for changes. Dufour and Eaker write that continuous improvement, a persistent discomfort with the status quo, and a constant search for a better way characterize the heart of a professional learning community. Continuous improvement requires that each member of the organization be engaged in considering several key questions (1998, 28).

1. What is the fundamental purpose?
2. What do we hope to achieve?

3. What are our strategies for becoming better?
4. What criteria will we use to assess our improvement efforts?

We continued to engage in dialogue about what outcomes were needed as a result of an improvement plan that would lead to an effective literacy program. The list was rather lengthy but realistic as to what a school reform should do. The following is what everyone agreed upon: increase reading/literacy achievement, reduce the percentage of students in the bottom quartile, increase the percentage of students in the third and fourth quartiles, narrow performance gaps, decrease student retention, decrease discipline problems, enhance students' self-esteem and self-motivation, raise expectations from teachers, increase student attendance, and incorporate best teaching practices and techniques.

Data revealed that we had more students in the lower quartile in literacy than in the third and fourth quartiles, which meant there was a high percentage of students who could be looked at for retention. When a school is looking at retaining fifty or more students in first and second grades, it presents an unpleasant picture of that school's performance and instruction. Many of our students came to school lacking in skill readiness, and with the diverse range it was difficult for teachers to effectively reach students at every level of performance. Teachers do the best they can, but sometimes even they need help in accomplishing their goals. Therefore, looking at a nongraded primary system in which students progress according to readiness seemed very practical. We needed a program where students don't have to be labeled by grade and where they can excel to their potential if given a chance to develop. Students who are advanced and in the top quartile can continue to excel and not be held back waiting for others.

I looked at how we could link literacy development to the continuous progress approach. Once grade-level designations are no longer in place as barriers, continuous progress can take place as students develop. Continuous progress within grade levels just doesn't seem to have the same impact. Teachers could see the connection but were leery about the process of putting this program in place. I continued to stress that whatever we decided, we would work closely as a team and I would make sure they were given all the support needed to accomplish the plan in a professional and effective way.

Teachers

It is not as difficult to get teachers' support for change as it is to get support from some parents. This is not to say I received immediate support from my teachers, because I did not. It took some convincing and a lot of discussions. As more and more information was shared about the plan of action, I asked teachers and staff to allow their minds to act as a parachute: you open it for a safe landing, but when you try to land with it closed, you are heading for a fall.

When I shared achievement data with teachers, they were shocked because no one had put it all together as bar graphs on charts and discussed it as schoolwide performance. Usually the most common response when teachers see low data is to blame the students and talk about all the outside forces that hinder their learning. But this did not happen as a result of viewing our data. The teachers were more attuned to how the problem could be fixed. The concern that most expressed was the many levels of performance in their classrooms. They talked about how their entire day was instructing reading and math. Math has a short block of time because by the time they finish instructing several different reading levels every day, it leaves a short time frame for other disciplines.

One of the questions I asked teachers is, who do you plan your lessons around? I wanted teachers to be candid with their responses because if we were going to make changes to what was not working, we needed to know what had kept achievement low. One teacher answered, "I plan my reading instruction for the middle (average) students." My next question was, how do you address students on other levels such as below average and above average? Her honest response was that she hoped the below-average performers would pick up as instruction is going on, and that the above-average students get more challenging worksheets to complete and can help the struggling students or go to the library and complete a research topic. As discouraging as these answers were, they were honest ones. My goal in meeting with teachers at this point was to encourage dialogue like this in a nonthreatening environment. Knowing where we were helped us to better understand where we needed to go.

The fact that no overreaction or criticism was seen on my part helped me build a trusting relationship with my teachers. What must be foremost in the school administrator's mind when seeking support for change is that unless those involved can feel a sense of support and trust, change is not going to occur. People will not change because you say they need to. Teachers must be involved in the decision-making process from the beginning. They must embrace the need to change based on solid data and information. Teachers must know they are not going to be left alone. And, finally, they must be convinced that the reform will make a positive difference.

Even though our dialogue sessions provided many answers, I decided to develop a survey for teachers to respond as candidly as they had during our open sessions. This would give other teachers who still may have been uncomfortable in open sessions the chance to express themselves and provide additional input, giving them the opportunity to think through questions and concerns that may not have been addressed. I needed to know the level of their knowledge of the continuous progress approach. Some of the questions on the survey were as follows: What is your knowledge of the continuous progress concept? What questions do you have that will help you better understand it? Do you feel this program concept will address our needs? Why or why not? Once the surveys were completed, the questions and answers were compiled and shared with the staff. I could sense that the survey helped alleviate some anxiety among teachers and staff because it was a way of reiterating that their opinions and questions were important.

McEwan (2003) writes, "Effective instructional leaders recognize the importance of sharing the responsibility for developing the vision, making decisions, and implementing programs" (2003, 24). According to McEwan, (2003), Lightfoot (1983) highlights the importance of teachers:

> In these good schools the image is one of teachers with voice and vision. Teachers are knowledgeable and discerning school actors who are the primary shapers of the educational environment. They are given a great deal of autonomy and authority in defining the intellectual agenda, but their individual quests are balanced against the requirement that they contribute to the broader school community. Most important, good schools are places that recognize the relationship between the learning and the achievement of students and the development and expression of teachers. (2003, 102)

Parents

As with teachers and staff, parents exhibited mixed feelings about instituting the continuous progress approach to improve literacy achievement. I scheduled several meetings for parents to engage in dialogue with me and my teachers. In order to accommodate all parents, meetings were scheduled during the school day and in the evening. At the very first meeting with parents, I shared the same information and achievement data that I had shared with the teachers. Reactions were mixed: some were unpleasantly surprised, some were a little angry due to unawareness, and so forth. Parents asked how and why this had happened. They wanted answers and wanted to know how it was going to be fixed. At this point I presented a plan for implementing a continuous progress approach. The idea of removing grade designations at the primary levels was the most controversial, as I expected. Performance grouping did not cause as much of a reaction.

I let parents know that no final decision had been made and there would be more meetings before we made a decision. I sent articles to parents about continuous progress approaches in other schools and the research on it in general. I kept parents informed by sending more information about the process prior to subsequent meetings, which gave them an opportunity to ask questions about what they were reading. As parent meetings continued, I sent surveys home to get written reactions from parents. The parent survey contained questions such as, What questions/concerns do you have about the proposed program? If this program is implemented, what can the principal and teachers do to help relieve any anxiety you may have? Would you be willing to support this program if you felt it will benefit all children in reading and language development?

As stated in an earlier chapter, the school board required a waiver request when schools deviate from traditional programs. Prior to the board's discussion and vote, I engaged parents and community members to voice their opinions and comments. During this session, some parents addressed the board in support, while others dissented. Jontz-Merrifield, reporter for the *Potomac News*, wrote this headline, "School's no-grade plan riles parents" (1997, A1). At this same meeting, many of my teachers commented in support and shared their rationale as classroom teachers. What I did find out is that some parents who spoke in opposition thought that the concept of nongraded meant having no letter grades on report cards even though it had been explained many times in meetings and in the literature sent home. Once this misconception was dispelled, some of the oppositional parents came to support the program. In the meantime, I kept an open-door policy for parents to meet with me individually if they felt the need to. In the end, the school board voted to grant me approval to implement the continuous progress approach to increase our literacy achievement.

Central Office

Before I could request a waiver from the school board, I needed to gain support and approval from the district superintendent. The superintendent could let me know if he felt this program was a plausible solution to my school's literacy challenges. Because my superintendent had a strong instructional background, he was able to listen with an open mind. One factor I wanted understood was that if the program was approved, I could not make it successful alone. It would take serious commitment and motivation from the teachers involved. Teachers could not be pulled along, nor could I spend time trying to motivate their interest. Having shared this with the superintendent, I asked for teacher and staff options.

The superintendent agreed, and he and my area superintendent suggested talking with teachers and giving them the option, on an individual basis, to transfer to another school within the district that would be more aligned with their educational belief and philosophy. On the other hand, there might be teachers at other schools that could support and commit to our school's new philosophy. His suggestions were encouraging for the success of the program. I proceeded to work through this with teachers. In summary, school leaders are more apt to support innovative school reform when you have done your homework and present a rationale that is solid and supported by data (qualitative or quantitative).

Students

The primary students were the most flexible group to work with during the implementation of our program. After all, being in school is a new experience for many primary students, especially kindergarten and first-grade students. Many of the parents of incoming first-graders attended meetings during the students' kindergarten year regarding the change in the school program. Therefore, many parents had already explained the new program to their children. Students who would technically be going into traditional second grade had to make the biggest adjustment to the new program. They had spent their first year of their school experience in self-contained graded classrooms. The experience of saying "I am in Mrs. Brown's primary" versus "I am in first grade" was new to them. Knowing they would have a chance to move to other primary levels in a few months was also a change for this group. At the end of the year before implementation of the program, teachers explained to their students what the program was about and what changes would take place. They also set aside time for students to ask questions, no matter how simplistic. I was sure many primary students did not have full understanding of the change. My belief was that the understanding would become clearer once they were physically involved during the upcoming school year. Teachers presented the program idea in an enthusiastic manner to get students excited about the change. We saw many students' excitement at the end of the year. They all seemed to look forward to a new experience in the fall.

ESTABLISHING AN EFFECTIVE SCHOOL CULTURE

A school's culture is impacted by its vision and mission. Reorganizing our school program to improve literacy achievement meant establishing a culture within our school that would enable us to successfully accomplish our mission. A school's culture is more than its climate. Climate is a part of the culture in a school or organization, but it is not the ultimate component. The culture in my school did not give a sense of productivity prior to the reform process. There was no sense of collegiality, professionalism, or high expectations for student success. In order for our reform process to successfully show improvement, the culture of our school had to change. The culture of a school should reflect its values, beliefs, and norms.

As Deal and Peterson write, "School cultures are complex webs of traditions and rituals that have been built up over time as teachers, students, parents and administrators work together and deal with crisis and accomplishments (Schein, 1985; Deal and Peterson, 1990). Cultural patterns are highly enduring, have a powerful impact on performance, and shape the ways people think, act, and feel" (1999, 4).

Deal and Peterson note, "More recently, numerous studies of school change have identified the organizational culture as critical to the successful improvement of teaching and learning. . . . Study after study, where the culture did not support and encourage reform, that improvement did not occur. In contrast, improvement efforts were likely in schools where positive professional cultures had norms, values, and beliefs that reinforced a strong educational mission. Culture was a key factor in determining whether improvement was possible" (1999, 5).

According to Brown and Moffett (1999), Saphier and King (1985) write, "School improvement emerges from the confluence of four elements: the strengthening of teachers' skills, the systematic renovation of curriculum, the improvement of the organization, and the involvement of parents and citizens in responsible school-community partnerships. Underlying all four strands, however, is a school culture that either energizes or undermines them. Essentially, the culture of the school is the foundation for school improvement" (117).

There are twelve cultural norms linked to school success as identified by Saphier and King and noted by Brown and Moffett (1999), as follows:

- Collegiality
- Experimentation
- High expectations
- Trust and confidence
- Tangible support
- Reaching out to viable knowledge bases
- Appreciation and recognition
- Caring, celebration, and humor
- Involvement in decision making
- Protection of what's important
- Traditions
- Honest, open communication

Through my personal experience in school reform, the norms listed above must occur for improvement to occur. As principals, we must take the lead in ensuring that these norms are incorporated into our school improvement plans.

Developing a Shared Vision

One of the first tasks for bringing teachers and staff together as a professional learning community is to develop a shared vision. It is almost impossible for change or school reform to effectively take place without shared vision. The process should be structured and taken seriously by all involved.

Once I knew the final decision was made to implement an improvement plan, my first task was to develop our own schoolwide vision statement, one that would be supported by all involved and give us a common direction toward our improvement process. My goal in working with my teachers and staff to come up with a shared vision statement was to make certain everyone actively participated in its development and that everyone clearly understood the meaning behind the statement. My rationale stemmed from Senge's statement that "there are two fundamental sources of energy that can motivate organizations: fear and aspiration. The power of fear underlies negative visions. The power of aspiration drives positive visions. Fear can produce extraordinary changes in short periods, but aspiration endures as a continuing source of learning and growth" (1990, 225).

I did not want a sense of fear remaining with teachers and staff after we agreed on our vision. Everything had to make sense and be clear without question marks. This is why we needed to show support for diverse comments and ideas and work to shape these into a common understanding. The fact that our process began by asking everyone to write their own personal vision statement was a step toward showing support for all opinions and ideas. We tried a structured approach where everyone knew the process and knew that it would take time to come up with a finished product that we could all live with and support.

Our process developed in five steps. First, every staff member was asked to write three or four statements about his or her beliefs and vision as related to our school reform. Second, staff worked in small groups to share their statements with one another. The task of each small group was to agree on a four-line paragraph that represented the group's thinking. Third, each small group presented their statement to the whole group. Discussion took place to eliminate redundant statements and to identify key words and statements that would describe everyone's beliefs and what they were committed to do. Fourth, once a statement was developed and agreed upon, a committee was formed to finalize the wording of what people had agreed on. Fifth, the committee presented the final written vision and mission statements for a vote by the entire staff. Once the vision statement was agreed to by all, I made copies and had them framed for each teacher. The vision statement was displayed in every classroom, the hallway, and the office area. It was visible to everyone, which is the way it should be. Often, schools' vision statements are displayed only in the office and sometimes in the hallway.

Fullan notes (from Deal and Peterson, 1994), "Developing a shared vision for the school can motivate students, staff, and community alike. It is not simply for the leader, it is for the common good. By seeking the more profound hopes of all stakeholders, school leaders can weave independent ideas into a collective vision" (2000, 205).

Our five-step process took us about four to six weeks to complete. Our completed vision statement reads,

We envision our school to be an outstanding school, one which challenges each student to reach his or her potential. Students will receive individualized instruction and will continually move forward in their learning. Opportunities will be provided for collaboration among students, teachers, parents, and community. We will ensure a safe learning environment where students can acquire knowledge and develop critical thinking skills needed to succeed in our changing, culturally

diverse, and technological world. We will have the highest expectation for our students and we will support the unique qualities each
person contributes to our school.

Our mission statement stated, "Our school will establish a learning environment with instructional focus on developmentally appropriate practices, integrated curriculum, cooperative learning groups,
multicultural learning experiences, varied and ongoing assessments,
developing critical thinking skills, and effective use of instructional
technology."

Your vision statement says who you are and what you are about.
The development process alone made a positive difference in how
my teachers and I related to each other. It was a collaborative
process that caused us to come together as individual professionals
and develop into a professional unit.

According to Glickman,

> Any successful organization, whether it is a community or a religious,
> social, business, or education group, has a set of core beliefs that
> holds its individual members together. That set of beliefs transcends
> any one person's self-interest. In the long run, the core beliefs help the
> group accomplish its mission and fulfill the needs and aspirations of
> individuals. The transcendent beliefs of successful groups do not sim-
> ply force individual members to comply with the group; rather, they
> are developed from the members' ability to accomplish together what
> they could not do alone. Group goals become the ultimate fulfillment,
> both of the collective and of the individual. (1993, 15)

Creating a Collaborative School Community

An essential element that determines the success of a school's improvement plan is the creation of a collaborative environment. It is
most important for survival of any organizational improvement plan.
There has to be a sense of collegiality among and between all stakeholders. One method of starting a collaborative environment is the

team approach. In fact, having the willingness to work in a team-oriented school environment was mandatory for teachers and staff interested in working in the continuous progress school. Defining team learning was the first step. Some people assume working in a team environment means team teaching together in a classroom. That was not at all the meaning behind the team approach I sought to develop and implement. My idea of team learning was to develop a school culture where teachers and staff exchange dialogue, materials, resources, and ideas; bond as professional experts with respect for diversity; and share positive energy in everything they set out to accomplish.

According to Senge,

> Team learning has three critical dimensions. First, there is the need to think insightfully about complex issues. Here, teams must learn how to tap the potential for many minds to be more intelligent than one mind.
>
> Second, there is the need for innovative, coordinated action. Outstanding teams in organizations develop the same sort of relationship—an "operational trust," where each team member remains conscious of other team members and can be counted on to act in ways that complement each other's actions.
>
> Third, there is the role of team members on other teams. Though it involves individual skills and areas of understanding, team learning is a collective discipline. (1990, 236–237)

Teachers and staff were engaged in dialogue as to how we would define the team concept in our school as part of our improvement plan. We agreed that our first start to implementing our team concept was to change from using "I" to using "we." Working in isolation was no longer an option. Teachers and staff had to find ways to engage in professional dialogue and come up with plans for working together. Teachers had to attend bimonthly team meetings. Each team was asked to choose a facilitator. I initiated dialogue by developing a team minutes form that had to be completed at the end of each meeting with a copy given to me. The team minutes form had sections for discussion, instructional issues, administrative issues and questions, and miscellaneous (lists of team events/field trips, programs, etc.).

Teams were made up of diverse groups of people. Diverse groups bring diverse ideas and values. As part of team learning and discussion, teachers were made cognizant of this and discussed how important it would be for every team to acknowledge differences of opinions as a means to an effective collaborative approach. We agree to disagree, and that is how team learning strengthens everyone. Part of a team's function in a collaborative environment is to show mutual respect for differences of ideas, questions, and comments. My statement to encourage collegiality was that if one person is talking and sharing ideas, then only one person is doing the thinking. The teachers' biggest task was to learn how to come to consensus. Consensus does not mean that you totally agree but that you can support the decision. This is how effective teams handle decision making, and you find as time goes on that this process becomes easier.

The structure of our program requires teachers to work collaboratively with all teachers within their teams and across teams. The success of the program is dependent upon teachers' knowing what instruction is taking place in all levels of instruction. Accuracy of student placement on the continuum depends on teachers' decisions. Teacher dialogue with other teachers is not optional regarding student data and achievement. This is the thrust of our program's goal to increase student achievement.

Implementing the team concept enhanced the culture within our school. When you walk into our school, you feel a sense of unity. The greatest impact was seen in our students' perception of the school. They appeared more connected to the school, which increased their willingness to learn more.

Another factor that enhanced our creation of a collaborative environment was open dialogue that occurred between teachers, staff, and me. I made every effort to support teachers in their learning and working through our school improvement plan. Teachers met with me individually once a quarter to discuss the performance data of students in their levels. This was done in a nonthreatening environment where we shared professional dialogue about what was working for them and what changes, if any, needed to be made. I always kept our discussion tone at a level of interest and support. I wanted teachers to leave our discussions with positive thoughts and reenergized to continue moving forward.

Another way team learning was improved was by the use of team programs. Each team was responsible for a program during the school year that engaged all students in some area of creative performance. These program goals lead to teams' working closely with students across their team levels.

Senge writes, "Individual learning, at some level, is irrelevant for organizational learning. But if teams learn, they become a microcosm for learning throughout the organization. Insights gained are put into action. Skills developed can propagate to other individuals and to other teams (although there is no guarantee that they will propagate). The team's accomplishments can set the tone and establish a standard for learning together for the larger organization" (1990, 236). As school leaders, we have to take the first step in creating a collaborative, collegial environment for our teachers to work effectively and for our students to learn effectively.

After the first year of continuous progress implementation, teams were asked to share their experience with the program by writing comments we could share with parents in our school newsletter. Team one wrote, "The best thing about Continuous Progress for us as a team has been the strong sense of collegiality that has developed among faculty. We have delved into the curriculum in order to best fit it together with the other pieces of the puzzle (instruction and performance assessment). We feel Continuous Progress has helped all teachers learn about themselves as teachers and know each student as fully as possible in order to teach him or her in the best way possible."

Team two wrote, "All of the children are finding success in literacy at their level of performance. The academic needs of the children are better accommodated through more effective planning. There is no longer a wide range of performance abilities that were difficult to plan for within one classroom. The teachers are more aware of students' academic performance."

Team three noted, "Teaming and carefully planning through the components of continuous progress, task centers, cooperative learning, vocabulary development, and thematic instruction have allowed team three to grow professionally, and this in turn rewards the children in our classes, within our team. Additionally, goals are set within our curriculum and the strategies for teaching those goals are made developmentally appropriate for each of the classes. This program allows us to focus on individual needs of students while establishing goals for increased student academic performance."

Schlechty writes,

Change requires commitment of energy and resources. It requires people to take risks and break habits. It causes discomfort and uncertainty. It creates needs as well as satisfies them. When undergoing change, people need more support and security than when their world is stable; these needs must be satisfied for substantial change to go forward. What the leader wants from the customer is commitment, enthusiasm, risk taking, and inventiveness. What the customer wants is to be assured that he or she is an honored participant (rather than a pawn to be manipulated), a respected intellect deserving of support, and most of all a valued colleague. Such values must always be satisfied if leaders are to lead. But in times of change, where stress is high and security low, these values rein supreme—and woe be to the aspiring leader who denies them. (1990, 95)

A committee was formed to work with me on developing a timeline for professional development, research, conferences, and so forth.

Professional development is a major component of our school reform process, and its effectiveness would determine the success of the program. Our timeline covered eighteen months of professional development, including some summer sessions. The written timeline provided everyone with direction for short- and long-term implementation.

Given the intensity and longevity of our eighteen-month professional development program, I created opportunities for teachers to attend some minisessions of professional development during the school day. At least once a semester, I arranged to have substitutes for teachers. For example, I had substitutes scheduled for two days. On day one, substitutes covered half a day for team one, and the team one teachers participated in a professional development minisession. The other half of the day, the substitutes covered classes for team two teachers while they completed their professional development minisession. The next day, team three attended their half-day session, and so on. Providing teachers with this opportunity reinforced both my support as a school administrator and the importance of their involvement in our school improvement plan. As Schlechty writes, "Those who would lead change in schools must be especially attentive to designing the changes and their implementation in ways that foster collegiality" (1990, 92).

Parent Involvement

As noted earlier, parents were divided in how they felt about our school reform movement. One group supported the changes even if they did not clearly understand them, one group was totally against the changes and worked hard to block them, and one group did not have a strong opinion either way. The latter group is where I put additional energy to gain their support as recommendations were made to the school board for a program waiver. In any case, we had stronger parental support for our school improvement plan than not.

My task did not end with gaining support for our program; the real task was maintaining support and getting parents involved in the school so that they could see firsthand the positive outcome of the changes and also so that their support and presence would enhance our students' perception of the importance of school and learning. As you recall, the reason for the reform was to get our student achievement up from the bottom. Data showed that our students, especially in the primary grades, were literacy deficient, and their performance was years behind expected development. A high percentage of our parents were not involved in the school and their children's learning. A small percentage of parents were engaged in the school and student learning. Students of many of this small percentage of parents were achieving as expected. We found that many (not all) of the students whose parents were less engaged in the school and learning were not achieving as expected. Therefore, we incorporated a parent involvement component in the school improvement plan. We felt that getting the uninvolved parents involved would help decrease student discipline problems and increase our low student attendance rate. Informational meetings throughout the school year inviting parents to attend during our development and implementation stages were our initial step in getting parents involved and knowledgeable about what was going on in their child's school and why their child's school was unique among schools in the district.

Once the continuous progress program was in place, we continued with informational meetings about it, but we worked on other ways to get and keep parents positively involved in our school beyond PTO boards and advisory councils. One change that pleased parents and received positive feedback was that teachers took the time to share and discuss with parents their children's achievement data. Every student had an assessment portfolio that teachers shared with parents. Performance data such as miscue analysis results (for primary students), Gates-McGinitie assessment results (for intermediate students), writing assessments, and math evaluations are part of assessment portfolios. Teachers reviewed each child's results with parents and gave suggestions for continued improvement. Because the continuous progress approach places students at their perform-ance or success levels, parents could see the progress their children were making.

This was very encouraging for parents, especially parents who were used to receiving negative reports about their children's progress. In fact, we kept count (by parent sign-in) of how many par-ents attended conferences because our goal was 100 percent atten-dance. In trying to meet this goal, we saw an increase in attendance each parent-teacher conference period. I believe that as the word spread about the information and positive comments parents were getting during conferences and from student data, more parents felt comfortable attending.

Another strategy put in place to increase parental involvement was setting aside a day for an open house. During the first year of program implementation, we held an open house day in the spring. This meant parents were invited to school in scheduled time blocks (to accommodate numbers in classrooms) to sit with their children and observe how and what they were learning. I wanted our first open house to take place during this first year because I wanted par-ents to see how "normal" our classes looked and how everyone in-teracted in teaching and learning. The uniqueness of our program, even though it received support for implementation, still left ques-tion marks in people's minds as to how it actually would operate. Parents could leave the open house with a little more ease about their children's unique educational program and therefore could share with the community the fact that their students were learning.

We held literacy and math family nights twice a year. Parents at-tended with their children. Teachers and reading specialists provided materials and resources for parents to make a learning activity and take it home to work with their children. After parents finished mak-ing the activity, teachers demonstrated its use. Parents and children had the opportunity to work together during the session. This be-came a big success, and these sessions were well attended by parents and students.

According to Deal and Peterson,

> School performance and parent involvement are intimately inter-
> twined (Levine and Lezotte, 1990). Having parents involved in
> schools can narrow cultural gaps that arise when parents are held at
> arm's length or feel apathetic toward school or their children's learn-
> ing. Only when a solid and positive partnership prevails between
> schools and parents will education flourish. The community ex-
> changes many things with the school. Schools need strong, organic
> linkages between schools and parents. They need parents who see the
> importance of schools and impart this to their children. On the other
> side, parents need schools that understand their perspectives and help
> them with their children. (1999, 132)

PROFESSIONAL DEVELOPMENT THROUGH
REFLECTIVE PRACTICE

The terms *professional development* and *staff development* are used
interchangeably throughout this section. One of the primary reasons
for our program's success was the strong professional development
program put in place as a component of our school reform. I wanted
a professional development model that was comprehensive and
where learning would be a sustained experience. What most people
usually get from staff development is a brief session of meaningless
research or experiences. There is never accountability or opportunity
for trial and error; therefore, once the session is over, so is the experience. I wanted accountability and learning by experience to be a
part of our professional development program, so I included reflective practice as part of our model. Professional development sessions
must be developed around the school's instructional program according to strengths and needs of teachers and staff if learning is to
be sustained and student results are to be achieved.

Sparks and Hirsh (1997) state,

> Educational reformers argue that reform efforts must be more school
> centered. This emphasis, however, meets a barrier in districts where

staff development is district driven. Curriculum coordinators in these districts, for instance, update elementary teachers on new materials, and district staff developers provide training in generic instructional techniques such as cooperative learning. Although such districtwide awareness and skill-building programs have their place within a comprehensive staff development program, more attention today is being directed at helping schools meet their specific goals for improved student learning. (1997, 33)

In developing our professional development plan, I made sure it had some connection to our districtwide staff development goals. Many of the district goals focused on areas of literacy; therefore, it was not difficult to align the plan with those goals.

Many times when practitioners mention reflective practice as a means of professional development, some redefine this process according to individual conceptions. I think of reflective practice as having an opportunity to put into action what is learned and being able to evaluate and adjust according to needs and expectations to obtain specific learning outcomes. According to Osterman and Kottkamp,

Reflective practice is located within the older tradition of experimental learning and also the more recently defined perspective of situated cognition. Experimental learning theorists including Dewey, Lewin, and Piaget maintain that learning is most effective, most likely when it leads to behavioral change, when it begins with experience and specifically problematic experience. From experience and research, we know that learning is most effective when people become personally engaged in the learning process, and engagement is most likely to take place when there is a need to learn. (1993, 20)

While working to overcome barriers put forth because of the program's unique and nontraditional structure, we had not focused on the best approach for teaching literacy at assigned skill levels. Teacher training in effective teaching strategies was a priority if we were to close achievement gaps. The most effective way to train teachers in instructional techniques that they can research, learn, and put into practice is through a reflective practice model. I wanted accountability to be a part of the professional development model. If teachers are to maintain and continue to use what they learn, they need to see support from school administrators, especially if we have designated specific sessions as mandatory instructional strategies for increasing student achievement.

Reflective Practice Plan

The more structured the approach for professional development, the more effective the learning outcome. Teachers were aware that our professional development plan involved a different process than had been the norm. My goal was to provide training and information that was relevant and could be put immediately into practice. Reflective practice was key to our development and implementation of professional development. The fact that we were going through school reform meant that our professional development topics were identified up front. For example, schoolwide implementation of cooperative learning was one of our instructional techniques to enhance student achievement, so all teachers and staff received professional development on cooperative learning. Word study and vocabulary development was another instructional area where all teachers and staff received training because it was a schoolwide instructional technique identified for implementation. Other sessions included balanced literacy, flexible grouping, how to teach writing as an instructional process, and so forth. Teachers received professional development in every instructional strategy and technique identified in our improvement plan as a means of increasing literacy achievement. Our professional development process was designed as reflective practice approach. The design is a cycle of learning, collaboration, participation, observation, and implementation. The following process took place with each session or topic.

- *Research books and articles are identified for focus areas.* Teachers received books or articles relevant to the topic of their professional development. The purpose was to provide background knowledge about the topic that would enhance interest and understanding.

- *Teachers and staff read to become familiar with the material.* Since teachers were continuing with their daily instruction, they were given two weeks to read the material. If the material was a sizable book instead of an article, certain chapters were noted for reading.
- *The topic is presented as professional development.* At the end of the two weeks, teachers attended the actual training session. These sessions were presented by staff development professionals in particular areas or teachers within the school district or our school who were knowledgeable in these areas.
- *Interactive discussion and collaborative dialogue are a major part of the presentation.* Presenter and teachers engaged in feedback and discussion to broaden and strengthen their knowledge and skills.
- *Teachers are asked to put what was learned from the session into practice.* For example, if the session was about cooperative learning, teachers were asked to put it into practice upon returning to their classrooms.
- *Implementation takes place for the next two weeks.* During the implementation, a school administrator observed the practice in classrooms. This ensured that teachers were implementing the technique as planned, and it was a way to provide feedback and support for those who felt discomfort. Peer observation can also take place at this stage.
- *Teachers meet after the implementation period.* This session was considered feedback time. Teachers openly shared their instructional experiences from the implementation process. Instructional strategies and techniques are agreed upon and become a part of the schoolwide instructional program.

Osterman and Kottkamp write,

From experience and research, we know that learning is most effective when people become personally engaged in the learning process, and engagement is most likely to take place when there is a need to learn. In professional programs, for example, fruitful learning often doesn't begin until the person is on the job. Situated cognition focuses on both the process and the context of learning. In a view popularized by the recent attention to problem-based learning . . . situated cognition proponents maintain that learning is best accomplished through an active, social, and authentic learning process. Learning, they argue, is most effective when the learner is actively involved in the learning process, when it takes place as a collaborative rather than an isolated activity, and when it takes place in context relevant to the learner. (1993, 20)

As a school administrator, I made sure I attended every professional development session and participated along with teachers and staff. When schools go through a reform process, it is important for teachers and staff to view the administrator as being actively involved. Visibility and participation is important for continued interest and support. Having teachers as presenters increased team collaboration within our learning community. Every teacher was given a chance to work with other teachers as presenters. This created a professional atmosphere inside our school.

According to Sparks and Loucks-Horsley (1989), Stallings and Mohlman (1981) "determined that teachers improved most in staff development programs where the principal supported them and was clear and consistent in communicating school policies. Likewise, Fielding and Schalock (1985) report a study in which principals' involvement in teachers' staff development produced longer-term changes than when principals were not involved" (1989, 27).

Topics presented in our professional development sessions came from teacher and staff surveys. Of course our primary focus was literacy development, but we focused on math instructional strategies as well. Teachers completed surveys in March listing areas they felt needed more attention and training. The initial list of literacy seminars included balanced literacy (Au, Carroll, & Scheu, 1997), guided reading (Fountas & Pinnell, 1996), traditional phonics (Moustafa,

1997), and Words Their Way (Bear, Invernizzi, Templeton, & Johnston, 2000). Teachers received reading materials before these sessions were presented. These topics were presented over a course of thirteen months.

In addition to learning, as part of our professional development plan teachers received points that are required by our school district. This was a divisionwide point system to encourage teachers and staff to participate in professional development. Every teacher and administrator is required to have thirty staff development points by the end of each school year. This usually led to the type of situation discussed earlier: people went to sessions to get points, not the learning or experience. The district provided numerous topics for teachers to choose from, but none were taken seriously enough to put into practice; people merely wanted the points. To me, this was wasted time. My professional development sessions related to our schoolwide focus, and therefore learning went immediately into practice.

Another part of our reflective process was the evaluation component completed by teachers at the end of each seminar. We learned from these evaluations and adjusted sessions when needed. The reading material gave teachers and staff background knowledge prior to the presentation. You get a better sense of understanding when you can read, hear, and participate in learning.

Sparks and Loucks-Horsley note,

> In organizations where staff development is most successful, (1) Staff members have a common, coherent set of goals and objectives that they have helped formulate, reflecting high expectations of themselves and their students; (2) Administrators exercise strong leadership by promoting a "norm of collegiality," minimizing status differences between themselves and their staff members, promoting informal communication, and reducing their own need to use formal controls to achieve coordination; (3) Administrators and teachers place a high priority on staff development and continuous improvement; (4) Administrators and teachers make use of a variety of formal and informal processes for monitoring progress toward goals, using them to identify obstacles to

such progress and ways of overcoming these obstacles, rather than using them to make summary judgments regarding the "competence" of particular staff members (Conley & Bacharach, 1987); (5) Knowledge, expertise, and resources, including time, are drawn on appropriately, yet liberally, to initiate and support the pursuit of staff development goals. (1989, 26)

In essence, professional development is crucial to the success of any school reform process. You should have a well-developed plan for effective and long-lasting results. The bottom line is, the purpose for professional development is to share in a common goal, and that common goal is to improve student achievement through improved teaching practices.

PUTTING IT TOGETHER

You will read about the different components that go into organizing an effective continuous progress approach to literacy achievement in the primary grades. Each component is presented separately to provide the reader with detailed insight about its relevance to the reform process. I write as candidly as possible about the steps taken throughout this reform because even though we achieved outstanding results, it was not without working hard and overcoming barriers. There were times when I questioned whether or not we should continue, but each time this thought entered my mind, it was erased with the thought that we were going through a short-term sacrifice for a long-term goal. That goal was to increase literacy achievement as the cornerstone for our students to become lifelong learners.

As stated earlier, the concepts of continuous progress, nongraded classrooms, performance grouping, looping, and individualized instruction are not foreign to the field of education. The focus on literacy development through the continuous progress approach is a commonsense approach in the primary grades. It is a lot easier to buy a package program than to reorganize a school to a different program and different way of thinking. A package program doesn't require many changes, if any at all. Therefore, no one has to think any differently than before.

As my school started this approach, I felt strongly about achieving positive results, but I never imagined the results would be of the magnitude that they were. In fact, when the program was in its implementation stages, the state SOLs were just becoming mandatory. Therefore, the development of our program to increase literacy achievement had nothing to do with the SOLs at that time. Our school was addressing a long-term literacy achievement problem, and the timing just happened to coincide with the mandate.

By the time our first group of team one students entered third-level instruction, the SOL mandate was in its second year. My first group of third-graders to take SOLs the year before had had only one year in the program because it was in its second year of implementation. This group's passing rate was 56 percent (70 percent is considered minimum proficient rate), which was an increase of 8 percent from the year before. The next group of third-graders was the first group of students who had spent three full years on the primary continuum. Their literacy performance scores validated our program's success rate with 96 percent passage in English, 92 percent in math, 88 percent in social studies, and 92 percent in science.

At this time, my teachers and I felt a sense of victory. We had taken the risk to try a nontraditional approach to increasing literacy achievement for our students, and the program proved to do just what we set out to do. High expectations and perseverance through the development and implementation stages helped close achievement gaps in literacy development.

In this section, I will go through components of this program approach in practice. The primary components that will be discussed are (1) teacher level assignments, (2) student placement/performance groups, (3) student assessment portfolios, (4) instructional techniques, (5) literacy skill levels, (6) peer observations, and (7) midyear movement.

Teacher Level Assignments

Teachers received training on how the hierarchy of literacy skills was developed by levels. They then had an understanding of how literacy skills for each level are sequenced for instruction. Levels on the continuum range from 1 to 9. The nine levels are divided into three teams. Team one has five levels (1, 2, 3, 4, 5), team two has four levels (6a, 6b, 7a, 7b), and team three has four levels (8a, 8b, 9a, 9b). The number of levels in each team is based on the number of students assigned to the team. Sometimes we had levels 3a and 3b in team one. The levels are in a hierarchy with specific literacy skill requirements for each level. I assigned teachers to teams. Team assignments were based on individual strengths and interests. Each team decides who will teach individual levels within the team. This type of teacher decision making enhances camaraderie.

This process gives teams a chance to discuss among themselves and reflect on their individual strengths in a nonthreatening professional learning environment. After level assignment decisions are made, each team submits its recommendations for approval. Level assignments for the upcoming year are decided in May of the previous year. Teachers have the flexibility to change levels each year or remain at the same level. This is a team decision and has worked out well. If a teacher changes teams, it is usually because of teacher transfer or relocation. When this happens, I always ask if there are teacher volunteers who want to change to the team opening. If no one volunteers, then I post a teacher vacancy for that position.

Student Placement

Student placement is decided twice a year (January and June). Placement decisions for newly enrolled students are made in August and September or whenever they enter throughout the school year. Earlier I discussed how students are placed in levels (classes) by performance and not by age. However, there is never a wide span in chronological age within performance groups. For example, if an eight-year-old's literacy performance is equivalent to a reading level of 1.0 (beginning first grade), this is a signal that there are other issues besides slow literacy development. A student this far behind in literacy development is recommended for further testing to determine the need for special education. Because continuous progress uses the approach to analyze student strengths and needs, I've seen a decrease in the percentage of students recommended for special education services. Providing students with instruction in areas where they show gaps has removed quite a few students from this identification process because our individualized quarterly assessments allow us to address many instructional issues before they become too serious. Most students lagging a year to a year and a half behind are considered slow learners. Slow learners need more time and more intense instructional strategies to make learning relevant. Once they receive this, slow learners generally make learning connections and start to move forward at a faster pace.

In May, teachers complete their third miscue analysis and their writing evaluations. Stanford results are usually received by the end of May. Teachers review and analyze data for individual students. They use this information along with what they observe during peer observations (discussed below) to make student placement decisions for the next school year. In addition, in the spring of each year, teams are given times to meet and make placement recommendations for all students moving to another team. For example, team one teachers meet to discuss students from levels 1 to 5 to make student placement decisions for team two levels 6a, 6b, 7a, and 7b. Not all students from levels 1 to 5 are considered for placement on team two because it is highly unlikely for a level one student to skip four levels of literacy skills by the end of a school year. Level one students are generally considered for movement to levels 3, 4, and possibly 5.

Team two teachers follow the same process for student placement on team three. Team three teachers group their students heterogeneously for fourth grade because students are literacy proficient by this point. This process can be tedious for kindergarten and teams one and two because they have to be as accurate as possible when placing students at literacy performance levels. They have the data, but they must also look at individual students' emotional, social, and independence levels. Much discussion takes place during placement meetings. The other part of student placement is that students do not move to levels as a group. Each student is looked at as an individual. For example, a level 5 teacher may recommend placement for his or her students anywhere within the four levels of 6a, 6b, 7a, and 7b on team two.

The program goal is to place students in an instructional environment where maximum literacy achievement and success can be obtained. Much weight in decision making is given to teachers. Sometimes teachers may have to review a student's data together and discuss their viewpoints. This process increases the professional bond between teachers. Teachers feel a sense of pride when their colleagues show faith in them by asking them to help make placement decisions.

Students new to our school are administered a miscue analysis and writing assessment before a placement decision is made. The reading teacher is responsible for assessing all new students. After new students are assessed, I meet with all new parents to explain our primary structure, discuss the test results, and recommend placement. To this day, I have not had a parent disagree with placement. In fact, most are impressed with the assessments and the dialogue about their child's literacy skills.

Speaking candidly about this part of my involvement, I enjoyed the dialogue with parents and felt this was a good way to start off with new parents in establishing a support system with them. But finding time for these meetings can be difficult because as the school administrator you still have responsibility for running the school. As the program became known and accepted, I was able to let my reading teacher and, when available, my assistant principal meet with new parents. If parents requested a meeting with me—and some did, of course—I always made myself available, and so did the assistant principal.

Student Assessment Portfolio/Accountability

As part of our program requirements, each student has an assessment portfolio. It does not become part of the student's permanent school record file, but it does go to the student's receiving teacher during midyear movement and at the end of the school year. Inside the student assessment portfolios are quarterly literacy assessments, quarterly writing evaluations and samples, and a copy of standardized test results. At the end of the school year, teachers leave only the last quarter's assessments and evaluations. This is the data receiving teachers analyze to make instructional decisions for the school year.

Each teacher has a class data analysis form that lists all students at their level and all assessment scores from student portfolios. This enables teachers and administrators to get a snapshot view of whole-level performance. Every quarter, teachers submit student portfolios along with their level data sheets. The assistant principal and I select and view at least five students' folders along with the data sheet that lists progress for all students for that teacher. Each quarter we select a different group of student folders to review. We provide written feedback to teachers on their group's performance, and if we see evidence of students lagging behind, we schedule a conference with that teacher to look at a plan of action to find out what is causing students to lag behind in performance.

Level data analysis sheets are very helpful to teachers because when you look at data in isolation, you don't get a chance to see the big picture all at one glance. With level data sheets, it is easy to see right away who is having trouble keeping up in the class, and it gives the teacher an opportunity early on to develop another strategy or improvement plan for these students. Written feedback to teachers shows our support as administrators for what they are doing instructionally and that we are there to provide assistance if needed.

Every June, teachers submit their level data sheets to me. Once data sheets are received, my office staff transfers the level data into bar graphs. The bar graphs compare fall, winter, and spring literacy data. The annual goal is for every level to show a minimum of nine months' growth in literacy development. For example, teacher A in level 2 (team one) has an overall class average of 0.68 in the fall of the year. In the spring this class's overall average in literacy development is 2.37, with a class growth of about 1 year and 7 months. Teacher B in level 6A (team two) has an overall class average in the fall of 1.78 and an overall class average in the spring of 2.68, with a growth of 9 months. This the minimum growth required for this teacher's class.

A data book is put together with the level data charts. Every teacher receives a data book at the end of the school year in which all teachers and staff can view schoolwide literacy performance data. This reinforces our school motto, "Continuous Progress Is Everyone's Responsibility."

Some of my colleagues asked how my teachers react to my sharing their data with other teachers. My response was, "We are all responsible for the achievement of students in our school. When our students perform poorly, we do not single out the problem as being because of teacher A or teacher B. We say it is the school's problem; therefore, everyone in the school is at fault. We are all here working together for a common cause, and just as we share in the positive, we must also share in the negative." In fact, teachers look forward to receiving these data books, and it does initiate instructional dialogue. The first year, teachers were a little leery, but the administrator has to set the stage, and I talked with teachers at the beginning of the year and let them know that the data books were for us to continue growth and not to evaluate individual teachers' performance because that is my job. We are here to show support for all colleagues. In actuality, I believe teachers really pushed to get their class performance up so they would not show a lack of progress when the data books came out.

Instructional Techniques—Best Practices

When we hear the word *literacy*, we think of reading, writing, and vocabulary building, which is correct. As part of our reform process, we sought to enhance what was commonly done in our teaching environment by involving our students in a variety of effective approaches to literacy achievement. Performance grouping provided teachers more time during their instructional day to include other effective teaching techniques in their learning environment.

As stated earlier, much of the school day in primary classrooms is taken up with instructing students at several performance levels in small reading groups because the developmental range in these classes is very diverse. Since our students were grouped by literacy performance, teachers had the latitude to effectively incorporate several instructional techniques. I will list the techniques and then discuss how teachers utilized each in their instructional day. Teachers used flexible grouping, vocabulary development and word study, the write-to-read process, task centers, and cooperative learning.

Flexible grouping is mandatory and an important technique to be used at every performance level on the continuum. You may think of flexible grouping and its effectiveness in the traditional classrooms with different performance levels, but it is just as effective in performance-level classes. For example, a level 3 (team one) class (six-year-olds) has seventeen students, and according to their entry assessment data, the students have a reading level of 1.5. To truly individualize instruction for these seventeen students, the teacher identifies from individual assessment data what specific reading skills (such as phonetic awareness or comprehension) each student shows as areas of deficiency. The teacher will regroup these students according to specific skill areas of need. Some students will master certain skills in a matter of days, while others will need more time and practice. As the teacher reassesses for mastery, he or she can regroup again to meet further instructional needs of individual students. Students are not locked into one reading group for three or four months. Teachers having narrow performance ranges in their classes can better utilize flexible grouping for individualization.

Vocabulary development is an instructional strategy that is implemented at all literacy levels on the continuum instead of a basic weekly spelling list. The rationale here is twofold. First, we want to increase student comprehension through word knowledge and understanding of context clues. Second, we know that a list of isolated spelling words has no true meaning unless students understand the meaning of the words in context. Third, isolated spelling words encourage rote memorization (low-level thinking) whereas vocabulary development encourages critical thinking at a higher level. Teachers could focus on daily or weekly reading words or spelling words; it was their choice according to what they wanted students to accomplish. However, the schoolwide rule was that these words must first be introduced to students in context. This enables teachers to focus on students' prior knowledge and use this prior knowledge as a way to increase their vocabulary development. Another strategy is for students to rewrite the vocabulary words in their own phrases or sentences. Everyone is familiar with the old weekly Friday spelling test of isolated words. Assessing spelling and vocabulary words in isolation was no longer a part of my teachers' instruction. When teachers make the decision to assess students on the vocabulary list, the words are read in sentences or phrases for students to write each sentence or phrase with the word in context. Teachers never call out isolated spelling words for students to write as a way of assessing students' ability to spell the words without conceptualizing the meaning of the words.

This was a longer process than just working with spelling lists for the sake of spelling, but the increase in students' comprehension and vocabulary use was amazing. The teaching of word study skills was part of literacy instruction. Students gained meaningful insight as to how words are related through patterns and meanings. Because word study is a developmental process and our students are grouped by developmental needs, the use of word study skills was easier to teach at the different performance levels.

According to Bear, Invernizzi, Templeton, and Johnston,

Word study is not a "one size fits all" program of instruction. One of the most unique qualities of word study is the critical role of differentiating instruction for different levels of word knowledge. Research over more than 20 years has established how children learn the specific features of words as well as the order in which they learn them.

Knowledgeable educators have come to know that word study instruction must match the needs of the child. This construct, called instructional level, is a powerful delimiter of what may be learned. Simply put, educators must teach to where a child "is at." (2000, 7)

Writing as a developmental process was how students received instruction in this discipline. Primary students (K–3) and intermediate students (4–5) were engaged in daily journal writing (a process of personal thoughts and choice). Teachers incorporated specific writing rubrics in their planning for instruction. These rubrics included composing (clear purpose, main idea, etc.), style (uses familiar vocabulary, sentence length, etc.), sentence formation (writes simple sentences, begins to expand, etc.), usage (uses adjectives, subject/verb agreement, etc.), and mechanics (capitalization, punctuation, etc.). There was either daily or weekly instructional focus of one of these rubrics, with the expected outcome that every student would demonstrate achievement in his or her writing skills as an effective means of communication.

Intermediate writing rubrics were more extensive than primary but covered the same areas. Students were assessed on specific areas of writing quarterly by receiving a topic to write about. All students on one team wrote about the same topic. Teachers evaluated students' writing according to the area of instruction for that period. Every student was to show improvement each quarter, with the ultimate goal of showing improvement in all rubric areas on their final writing at the end of the school year. Starting this writing process in kindergarten gave our students the writing skills they needed to pass the state writing test by fourth grade.

Task centers are another name for learning centers. We decided to use the word *task* because students would be undertaking a specific learning objective at each center. I suggested that each task center have a specific learning objective related to the current week's instructional goals or the previous week's (which could be a review of learning). Research tells us that every child has a dominant learning style. Task centers increase students' learning by allowing them to use all modalities for learning: visual, kinesthetic, and auditory. Task centers reinforce what children have learned or are learning. Instead of teachers constantly reviewing for mastery, task centers can take the place of this instructional task and allow students to actively and collaboratively engage in review for mastery as independent learners.

Cooperative learning is fostered by task centers. Most task centers are designed for small groups of students, usually two or three students working at the same task center. Task centers address reading, writing, math, and vocabulary skills. For example, if a teacher is working on blends (*bl, cr, sp*, etc.) in small-group direct instruction, a task center for the week includes a hands-on activity for reviewing these blends. A vocabulary task center activity can include writing vocabulary words in a sentence or highlighting vocabulary words in a paragraph. These are simplistic examples of how task centers can review instruction. Students enjoy the independence of working in center-based instruction.

Since task centers are set up for independent work (without direct teacher supervision), the teacher must have an effective management system in place. For example, my teachers set up a task center chart where students checked off a center when they completed the task. Usually teachers have five to six task centers for the week (manageable). We found that students could complete one to two task centers within the daily literacy instruction block. Task centers offer interesting hands-on learning activities that provide motivation for students to continue learning a specific objective. They also provide opportunities for students to make decisions and choices about what they are learning.

Cooperative learning is a technique that teachers implemented at all levels. Earlier, I mentioned that our school had not only instructional problems but discipline problems as well. Students did not get along and did not know how to work cooperatively in the learning environment. My teachers researched and received professional development about different ways to incorporate cooperative learning in their daily instructional program. Since students are performance grouped, teachers often used the cooperative learning approach with small instructional groups. Within each group, a student is responsible for a particular job task. For example, given an activity, students decided who would be the facilitator, the note taker, the artist, the spokesperson, and so forth. Students knew their individual evaluation came from the group's evaluation. Everyone in the group received the same grade. We started implementation of various forms of cooperative learning techniques in kindergarten, and it was mandatory that every teacher engage students in cooperative learning activities at least twice a week. Within a semester, we could see the positive difference this type of learning made with our students in how they started to show respect for one another and exhibited better social skills.

The first year was a little tedious for teachers in planning and closely monitoring cooperative learning groups, but after the first year and as students moved throughout performance levels, cooperative learning became a part of students' expectations; therefore, the teacher could take on the role of facilitator and move about the groups with less direct monitoring. According to Grant, Johnson, and Richardson, "An individual's quality of life as an adult depends largely on his social skills. Socially skilled people tend to be psychologically healthy. For these and many other reasons, we need to teach students skills necessary to build and maintain cooperative relationships with others (Johnson and Johnson 1989)" (1996, 9).

All the above techniques are instructional components that increased literacy achievement throughout performance levels. These were not optional techniques because of the need to maintain continuity as students moved through the continuum. If students in level 3 moved to level 5 in January, they would still engage in task centers, cooperative learning, flexible grouping, writing, and vocabulary development. It was important that all teachers on the continuum incorporated the same techniques, but how and when rested with the decision of individual teachers.

Literacy Skills Scope and Sequence

Our reading and language arts curriculum did not change as a result of restructuring. We did, however, alter the scope and sequence of these skills. Reading skills were listed in two sections, structural analysis and comprehension. A committee was formed to look at all reading and language skills in our curriculum. Skills were listed in a sequence where one skill builds upon another. For example, letter recognition is a beginning skill for reading, along with letter sounds. Identification and usage of long and short vowels need to follow, and blends should be a part of that sequence. Comprehension skills such as context clues, sequencing, story elements, and so forth should start in the early stages of reading instruction. We used this type of process to place skills at certain literacy levels. The symbols O, $+$, and X were used to indicate the levels at which a skill is introduced, the level at which it is maintained, and the level at which it should be mastered.

All teachers have the same charts so that a teacher can see what literacy skills students should have prior to entering their level and what literacy skills they are responsible for teaching and getting students to master. An example of how teachers may utilize these charts is as follows: For kindergarten, beside "rhyming words" is "O," meaning this skill is introduced here. Levels 1, 2, 3, and 4 have "+," indicating that teachers at these levels continue teaching rhyming words (maintaining). Level 5 has "X" by "rhyming words," meaning that mastery should take place there if not before. I will use team two for another example. "Vowel diagraphs" is listed under level 6a with "O" for introduction, while level 6b shows "+" for maintaining and level 7a shows "X" for mastery.

Teachers have the flexibility to use whatever resources are needed to teach their literacy skills for mastery. They can use basal texts (but not in isolation), children's literature, and other materials and resources. Professional development gave teachers a lot of strategies and techniques they could use, which enhanced their repertoire of teaching skills.

Peer Observations

Before midyear student movement meetings are held, teachers are given an opportunity to observe their colleagues at other performance levels. We call this peer observation. Student data are the major indicator of individual students' performance, but to make appropriate placement decisions for students moving into the next performance level, one must know where that performance level's instruction is taking place. This is done by collaboration and observation. During peer observation, teachers are able to see what and how instruction is taking place at other levels. Also, teachers can look at independence levels and emotional and social adjustments.

In January I designate a day for teachers on each team to observe, on a rotating basis, other levels they may be considering for their students to move into. For example, team one teachers observe team two levels. At least two teachers observe in any one class at a given time. For example, you may have two teachers in level 6a and two teachers in level 6b. At the end of the observation time (which is usually thirty minutes per level), the two teachers in level 6b go to 6a. Teachers observe students' work habits, look at work samples, which teachers usually have displayed, and view writing samples. The rotation goes very smoothly because teachers have ready-made schedules showing where they are going and at what time. The observer has a schedule of who is coming and at what time. Students are alerted in advance that teachers are coming to visit; therefore, they continue to engage in what they are doing.

The teachers' first experience with peer observation of this nature may have been a little uncomfortable, but as it continued, the teachers became more at ease, and they could empathize with one another because the ones being observed are also observers at other levels. Now, teachers had both quantitative and qualitative data to make placement decisions.

Midyear Student Progression

Midyear student movement occurs in January. Preparation begins in December. Teachers identify students at their levels for movement to another performance level and submit the list of names to the school administrator. Teachers complete a movement form for each student recommended for placement. The form asks teachers to list the receiving teacher (next performance level). The teacher has to write a brief prescriptive statement for each area of development: academic, social, and emotional. Usually for academic development a teacher may indicate reading level when entered and current level, whether the student is an independent worker, is task oriented, answers oral questions, uses appropriate level vocabulary, and so forth; for social development, whether the student enjoys group activities, gets along well with other students, is helpful, and so forth; and for emotional development, whether the student is always pleasant, is happy-go-lucky, is very sensitive, and so forth. The form includes a section to list assessment scores from quarterly assessments, writing evaluations, and the like. Teachers must indicate how and when they notified parents about the possibility of their child moving to another performance level. When teachers come to the meeting, they bring all assessments and work samples for each student recommended for movement.

Midyear movement decisions are made by a movement committee. This committee consists of administrators, the reading teacher or title 1 teacher, the guidance counselor, the school nurse (if necessary), the referring teacher, and the receiving teacher. Parents are invited to their child's meeting and are asked for input into the movement of their child. Every student referred to this committee is discussed as an individual. The referring teacher discusses the data and work samples with the committee. He or she elaborates on the student's social and emotional areas of development and shares why he or she selected the receiving teacher. Members of the committee can ask questions about any of the information presented. The receiving teacher especially is expected to ask questions because once placement is made, it is that receiving teacher's responsibility to continue moving the student ahead. Teachers do not have instructional time to drop back and catch students up on anything missed; therefore, the receiving teacher wants to make sure the student he or she is receiving can be successfully challenged.

Movement meetings can take up to two weeks depending on the number of students involved. During the first year I attended all movement meetings. Once the program was operating smoothly, I was able to be flexible in my attendance; however, a school administrator was always present.

Parents are sent a letter from the school administrator inviting them to attend the movement meeting. The teacher makes the initial contact. The letter indicates that their child has successfully mastered all the skills at their current level and upon recommendation of the teacher he or she is ready to move up to the next level of skills. It usually impresses parents to know their child is doing well and is meeting with success. I was very encouraged by the number of parents attending our movement meetings. It was even more special for those parents who in the past heard nothing but how poorly their child was performing to now be sitting in a meeting with school personnel and hearing how successfully their child is performing. At times it was emotional for some parents, and the tears shared by them in our meetings lightened our hearts as a professional staff.

During the movement meeting, parents ask questions about their child's performance, and they meet with their child's potential new teacher. After all information and data is shared, the committee votes on whether the student is ready for movement. Although parents are present during the vote, a follow-up letter is sent to parents, which they sign in agreement.

Continuous progress is an effective approach to literacy achievement. The change process takes some thought, time, and a genuine professional staff to make a difference. I believe that if all primary grades are restructured according to a continuous progress approach, literacy development will not be a primary concern in elementary schools. All students will be literacy proficient by third grade, and this national goal can be achieved and the question that has been lingering as to how to accomplish it will be answered.

INTERMEDIATE LOOPING AND CONTINUOUS PROGRESS

While the nontraditional primary structure places students in performance groups for literacy development, intermediate students (grades four and five) maintain a traditional approach to classroom grouping. However, in an effort to close learning gaps existing among intermediate students, I looked at the concept of looping.

Grant, Johnson, and Richardson describe looping as "a multi-year placement for both the students and the teacher" (1996, 4). An example is when our fourth-grade teacher takes her class to fifth grade and the fifth-grade teacher goes back to fourth grade to start a new multiyear class placement. Grant, Johnson, and Richardson state, "Numerous benefits accrue when a teacher stays with his students for more than one year: (1) Students have only half the teacher transitions, (2) The teacher has fewer parents with whom to relate over a longer period of time, (3) Attendance improves, (4) Overall, the discipline improves, (5) The curriculum becomes semi-seamless, (6) Learning time increases" (1996, 4).

Some schools that use looping as an approach to grouping give teachers the option of looping or not looping. Because I wanted to focus on looping to reap the benefits of a semi-seamless curriculum and increased learning time (as noted above by Grant, Johnson, and Richardson), teachers had to loop in grades four and five. Most were open to the idea, and a couple of teachers had reservations but were willing to give it a try. Once teachers tried looping with their students for one turn, they enjoyed the experience, but most importantly, they could see how it increased their instructional knowledge and skills. They could take students as far as they could go in the fourth- and fifth-grade curriculum. For example, if a fourth-grade teacher finds that his or her class can move into any part of the fifth-grade curriculum, they can do just that. Also, fourth-grade teachers know what students have learned and still need to know when they get to fifth grade. In a sense, looping is like continuous progress for students and teachers.

After one multiyear of looping, teachers shared some comments expressing their feelings about looping. Mrs. Brutski (fourth grade) wrote, "Looping will enable this year's fourth-grade class to enter fifth grade as a cohesive unit. As teachers we have had an opportunity to work with each other and we will know our students' strengths and needs. The students will have a rapport with their teacher and they will know the classroom climate before arriving at school. As a whole, we will be able to get down to the business at hand—learning!"

Mrs. Rogers (fifth grade) wrote, "It's been wonderful to have the same students two years in a row (looping). In social studies, I know what we covered last year so we just briefly review and move on to new content. It's such a help with pacing and time management."

Gaustad (1998) notes the benefits of looping: "Teachers and students in looping classes need not start from scratch every fall, learning new sets of names and personalities, establishing classroom rules and expectations. Most teachers find that students remain on task far longer at the end of the first year; accordingly, teachers estimate that they gain a month of learning time at the start of the second year." (1998a, 1).

Looping at intermediate levels offers flexibility for continuous progress as it allows teachers to move ahead without having a partition between fourth and fifth grades.

CHAPTER 4

Steps to a Successful School Reform

The steps below represent research and my personal experiences in the development and implementation of an effective school reform process. To eliminate any one step will weaken the results for successful completion of reform for any school or organization. In listing each step, I include an explanation and personal experience related to the process.

STEP ONE: IDENTIFY RATIONALE FOR REFORM

In order for any type of school reform to produce successful results, you must design a plan of action that will accomplish all goals and expectations. Often as educators we don't take time to develop comprehensive plans of action for changes we want made. Even though I worked in two different school divisions, each division had several changes in superintendents throughout my tenure. Changes in superintendents automatically mean changes in the way we do things. Divisionwide changes always focus on ways to improve student achievement.

What I most recall as a school administrator is being given directives to change, but rarely, if at all, were we presented with a structured plan for new development or implementation because the rule of thumb with most new school leaders is that they want to see these changes take place *yesterday*. When this is the case, people involved in making the changes happen tend to develop their own rationale for these changes, and this increases anxiety to levels where little commitment takes place. Sometimes when rapid changes occur, it is for the sake of the individual making the changes and not for the actual need to show improvement. When this happens, people directly involved spend a lot of wasted time criticizing the whys and hows of the change rather than actually going through the process.

Presenting solid research and data to all involved gives validity to any type of organizational reform. This helps eliminate time spent on lowering anxiety and uncertainty and gives you the opportunity to spend quality time on gaining commitment and support for an effective outcome.

Change in itself always yields discomfort at the beginning because people are asked to come out of their comfort zone. While it may be easier for some than others, change will always instill a level of discomfort. Student achievement has always been the basis for reform movements in school systems. Some of the most common changes are new reading programs, alternative grouping of students and classes, development and implementation of new teaching techniques, and changes in student and teacher evaluation measures.

When school reform is not supported by those who are directly involved in the process, you can expect problems to develop, and the expected outcome may never be seen. School reform means taking risks; however, risk taking can be minimized if you can show solid rationale. People in an organization are the ones who have to make changes, not the organization itself. If people are given a directive to change to a new system or program without clear evidence that the new way will produce better results than what is currently in place, they are more likely to resist.

In addition, reform can be costly, and how costly depends on the project. A great deal of funds from school division budgets goes into funding new programs and ventures that usually mean a cut of funds from another budget item. People want to know specifics like who is involved, what are they expected to do and when, and how much training is involved.

STEP TWO: ESTABLISH A SCHOOLWIDE SHARED VISION

The word *vision* has become the operative word in our educational system. It provides a focus and direction for schools. Establishing a school vision that is shared by all enhances collegiality among teachers, staff, and administrators. When there is a strong sense of collegiality in a learning environment, you will experience success and growth in just about everything you set out to accomplish.

Establishing a shared vision with my teachers and staff was the catalyst for our school reform. If we had not done so in the initial stage of our reform, our program would not have experienced the success that it did. It is hard to imagine a leader taking a staff through school reform with one vision while the staff members have totally different visions. Although this has happened many times over, you can rest assured that the school or organization did not achieve expected results.

When you share visions, it increases dialogue among all involved. It is energizing to collaborate with peers on a common interest and understanding. This will result in strengthening collegiality among staff. Soon after my teachers and staff completed our first vision statement, we could see as a group where we were going, and we were on the same page as to what actions we needed to take to get there. It is important to realize that the first vision statement is not a finished product but a start toward the end. Vision statements should change over time because you are not going to remain in the same place where you started out.

STEP THREE: SHAPE YOUR SCHOOL CULTURE

Vision impacts culture. For example, if you walk into a school or organization and feel it to be chaotic, unprofessional, or too loosey-goosey, you are in an environment that has not established a shared vision, and therefore the culture reflects just that. Prior to our reform movement, when you walked into our school building, you felt a sense of disarray. The staff lacked focus on teaching and learning, and they were involved in personal issues unrelated to school. Student discipline was out of control, and many students walked the halls.

Once my school developed its vision, the culture in our environment changed. It went from a feeling of chaos and unprofessionalism to a feeling of professionalism and collegiality. It is important to know that a school's culture defines who you are and what you are about. In essence, school culture impacts human behavior. I witnessed improvements in my teachers' and staff members' behavior that were not present prior to the cultural change. I observed teachers engaged in more instructional dialogue, they seemed more focused in their planning for teaching and learning, they showed mutual respect toward each other, and there was more sharing of materials and teaching techniques. I even observed changes in their appearance (dress code) and receptiveness to serve on school committees.

According to Deal and Peterson, "School cultures are complex webs of traditions and rituals that have been built up over time as teachers, students, and administrators work together and deal with crises and accomplishment (Schein, 1985; Deal and Peterson, 1990). Cultural patterns are highly enduring, have a powerful impact on performance, and shape the ways people think, act, and feel" (1999, 4).

STEP FOUR: IDENTIFY PROGRAM COMPONENTS IN NEED OF CHANGE

Research continues to reiterate that people do not change for the sake of change. If you want change to occur with positive results, people must feel confident that there is a need and clearly understand what kind of change is needed and why. Once you give them data that support a need to do something different, then you must present what that something different is going to be. In my situation, student achievement data supported a need to change our literacy program approach. At the same time as I discussed the need for change, I presented the alternative changes such as grouping, nongraded classes, a change in literacy instruction, and so forth. I communicated to teachers that we were looking at grouping our students differently, removing grade-level designations, and having a literacy program that included various instructional programs and techniques. All changes were clearly communicated to teachers and staff, both in writing and verbally. Having a clear knowledge of what is to come and how it is better than what you have will get support and interest from your teachers and staff.

STEP FIVE: DEVELOP A REFORM TIMELINE

A timeline is important for increasing support. I provided teachers and staff with a tentative timeline and the understanding that situations could arise that would impact projected dates and times but noted that we planned to stay as closely aligned to these dates as possible. The teachers got a sense of long-term planning and obligations, which gave them the flexibility to make other decisions. This was very insightful and helpful to my teachers and staff. In fact, sharing a timeline of events, meetings, training sessions, and activities gave them a sense of direction. They could see in the short term and long range where we were going and what we were going to do. We knew that things come up from time to time that would alter the time frame, but having some sense of what to expect allowed people to prepare and organize their minds.

Also, presenting the timeline offered the opportunity for teachers to give input and, if necessary, make alternate decisions. What I found most enlightening is that teachers and staff felt that I respected them as professionals because there were no hidden agendas. The timeline showed a year and a half of what was to come. The one-year timeline was not difficult to follow, but the next half year was difficult. Some things went smoothly and on schedule, and then there were some situations that did not go as planned and for which the timeline had to be altered. Therefore, I believe a nine-to-twelve-month timeline is adequate and can probably be followed as planned.

STEP SIX: DESIGN AN EFFECTIVE PROFESSIONAL DEVELOPMENT PLAN

As stated earlier, in any reform movement the organization does not change; people within the organization must change. In knowing this, we must provide a comprehensive plan for growth and development of all involved in the reform process. Change is a process that is usually sought for improvement within an organization. The organization will not improve without working to improve those who work within it. Professional development is too often unsuccessful in having long-term effects. One primary reason is the lack of connection to what the learning outcome is to be. A second reason is lack of familiarity with adult learning experiences. As school leaders, we can require our teachers and staff to attend professional development sessions, but we cannot mandate meaningful interaction and long-term results.

Professional development has to be a major component of any reform process; therefore, in our planning we must recognize that everyone is not going to be at the same level of need within the development process. This is the downfall for many of our professional development plans: we assume that everyone is at the same level of readiness, which is not the case. In knowing and working through individual needs and strengths, you are apt to get more support and interest from those involved. Support and interest will ensure positive results. My staff development plan proved to be successful among my teachers and staff because I did not make the assumption that everyone was at the same level of knowledge and interest in the area of developmental training. Those who needed additional support in the development process were given that extra time and support without making them feel inferior to other colleagues. The learning environment was always kept professional, collaborative, and supportive for all. This type of cultural atmosphere made it enjoyable to learn and maintained high levels of interest.

Using surveys prior to each planned session enabled me to make sure sessions were adjusted to meet the developmental levels of all involved. In fact, if there were teachers or staff members who noted high levels of knowledge and practice in certain areas, they became trainers for colleagues who may not have had those experiences and skills. We also made sure each session was relevant to specific teaching experiences and expected outcomes. Sharing of ideas and possibilities for alternative techniques was a part of each session's feedback.

According to the National Staff Development Council, "Successful professional development increases both independence and collaboration. It combines independent and interdependent learning approaches to facilitate the greatest possible growth. Identifying staff development outcomes is imperative. This produces clear expectations, which in turn improve results. Adults need to know the level of importance, the expected outcomes, and the rationale for recommended changes in their knowledge, attitudes, and skills. Adults are motivated by clear and measurable outcomes and ongoing support to sustain interest and ensure positive results" (1995, 17).

The most productive part of our professional development plan was incorporating the reflective practice approach. Even though it was time-consuming, it increased positive long-term results. Teachers were involved in the research part of each session by reading articles and books, they were involved in the presentation of information by interacting and building upon what they learned through reading, and they were able to actually put it into practice and evaluate and adjust it to their individual styles of teaching and learning. The effectiveness of this type of professional development—research, learning, practice, and evaluation—was beyond anything we could imagine.

STEP SEVEN: DEVELOP AN ASSESSMENT AND ACCOUNTABILITY PLAN

Determining the success of reform movements is crucial. We need to know if our changes are working. Are we being successful with what we are currently doing? Are the results what we want them to be? Do we need to increase, take away, or adjust? Many questions need to be answered when a reform process has taken place. We need to know results. With any reform process, there has to be accountability through assessment and evaluation. To bring about change with no monitoring system included is asking for failure.

According to Schlechty, "In education, there is an unfortunate tendency to assume that when performance is off there is a problem with performers. In a results-oriented evaluation system, the primary concern is to provide data that will make it possible to assess performance, determine the extent to which performance conforms with requirements, and where performance does not conform with requirements, provide a basis for determining why this is the case and what can be done to correct the problem. Performance evaluation seeks to solve problems; it is not intended to place blame" (1990, 113).

In my case, even though we knew our students' literacy achievement was very low, there was no immediate reaction to blame individual teachers and staff. My initial reaction was to look at the instructional program along with techniques and strategies. Did the instructional program fit our students' needs? This is the question I wanted answered before seeking other possibilities. What we found out in taking this approach was that our problems stemmed from the instructional program because our students' range of performance was so wide that the cookie-cutter approach was not working at our school site. Student performance data bought this to our attention. We found that our students were not benefiting from the program currently in place.

As we made changes through our reform process, we put in place quarterly student assessment measures along with annual performance evaluations to keep us informed as to how our program change was working and whether it was producing the results we wanted. Without an assessment and accountability plan, there is no true measure of outcome. Why continue working hard at something that is not producing the desired results? This is what happens when there is no way to measure how well you are doing.

As stated in the preceding chapters, change is never easy, but when you continue to get unwanted results from doing more of the same, it is time to look at doing something different. If you want change to produce expected results, you have to nurture the process through a well-developed and structured plan. You have to be patient as you work toward dotting every i and crossing every t. If you are looking for a quick fix to a problematic situation and you take a quick-fix approach, you will quickly revert back to receiving the same results as before.

In essence, my school achieved results above what was expected. This is not to say that expectations were not high; it is to say that our students' achievement in literacy came out above and beyond our already high expectations. Our reform process was very tedious, and yes, we were exhausted on many occasions from responding to continuous rebuttals about the uniqueness of our program, but yet people would say it made sense. We did not rush to get a quick fix: we knew it would take some time to see results. After one semester we saw a small increase in student achievement, at the end of the year we saw a greater increase in student achievement, by year two the increase was even greater, and by year three we had a 184-percent increase in student achievement in literacy compared to previous years.

As the school principal, I know that my teachers made the biggest difference in obtaining the results we now feel proud of. If I did not have teachers that were true believers and were willing to take a risk in being on the forefront of this innovative reform, our students would not have achieved the results they did. There are teachers who genuinely care and are willing to work hard to see students achieve success and be literacy proficient. My teachers and staff are proof of this.

References

Anderson, R., & Pavan, B. (1993). *Nongradedness: Helping it to happen.* Lancaster, PA: Technomic.

Au, K., Carroll, J., & Scheu, J. (1997). *Balanced literacy instruction.* Norwood, MA: Christopher-Gordon.

Bear, R., Invernizzi, M., Templeton, S., & Johnston, F. (2000). *Words their way.* Upper Saddle River, NJ: Prentice Hall.

Berliner D., & Biddle, B. (1995). *The manufactured crisis.* Reading, MA: Addison-Wesley.

Brown, J., & Moffett, C. (1999). *The hero's journey.* Alexandria, VA: Association for Supervision and Curriculum Development.

Carbo, M., Dunn, R., & Dunn, K. (1991). *Teaching students to read through their individual learning styles.* Boston, MA: Allyn and Bacon.

Deal, T., & Peterson, K. (1999). *Shaping school culture.* San Francisco: Jossey-Bass.

Dufour, R., & Eaker, R. (1992). *Creating the new American school.* Bloomington, IN: National Education Association.

Dufour, R., & Eaker, R. (1998). *Professional learning communities at work.* Bloomington, IN: National Education Association.

Dufour, R., Eaker, R., & Dufour, R. (2005). *On common ground.* Bloomington, IN: National Education Association.

Forster, L. (1999, September 17). "Two schools hold secret to SOL test." *Potomac News* (Woodbridge, VA).

Fountas, I., & Pinnell, G. (1996). *Guided reading.* Portsmouth, NH: Heinemann.

Fullan, M. (2000). *Educational leadership.* San Francisco: Jossey-Bass.

Gaustad, J. (1998). "Implementing looping." Eric Digest, Number 123.

Gaustad, J. (1992a). "Effective grouping practices." Eric Clearinghouse.

Gaustad, J. (1992b). "Nongraded Primary Education." Eric Digest, Number 74.

Glickman, C. (1993). *Renewing America's schools*. San Francisco: Jossey-Bass.

Goodlad, J. (1984). *A place called school*. New York: McGraw-Hill.

Goodlad, J., & Anderson, R. (1987). *The nongraded elementary school*. New York: Teachers College Press.

Grant, J., Johnson, B., & Richardson, I. (1996). *Multiage Q and A*. Peterborough, NH: Crystal Spring Books.

Grossen, B. (1996). "How should we group to achieve excellence with equity?" Retrieved from http://www.uoregon.edu/~adiep/grp.htm.

Hollifield, J. (1987). "Ability grouping in elementary schools." Urbana, IL: Eric Clearinghouse on Elementary and Early Childhood.

Johnson, R. (2002). *Using data to close the achievement gap*. Thousand Oaks, CA: Corwin Press.

Jontz-Merrifield, S. (1997, March). "School's no-grade plan riles parents." *Potomac News* (Woodbridge, VA), A1.

Joyce, B. (1999). "Reading about reading: Notes from a consumer to the scholars of literacy." *The Reading Teacher, 52*(7), 662–71.

Kulik, J. (1993). "An analysis of the research on ability grouping." Davidson Institute for Talent Development, Eric Digest.

Lortie, D. (1975). *Schoolteacher*. Chicago: University of Chicago Press.

McEwan, E. (2003). *7 Steps to effective leadership*. Thousand Oaks, CA: Corwin Press.

Manzo, K. (2005). "GAO to probe federal plan for reading." *Education Week, 25*(7), 22.

Moustafa, M. (1997). *Beyond traditional phonics*. Portsmouth, NH: Heinemann.

National Staff Development Council. (1995). *Standards for staff development*. Oxford, Ohio: Author.

O'Hanlon, A. (1998, June). "A measure of their success." *Washington Post*, p. 6.

O'Hanlon, A. (1997, April). "Triangle Elementary to group students by ability." *Washington Post*, p. 6.

Olson, L. (2005). "Impact of NCLB law on reading, math results debated." *Education Week, 25*(9), 22.

Osterman, K., & Kottkamp, R. (1993). *Reflective practice for educators*. Newbury Park, CA: Corwin Press.

Purkey, W. (1970). *Self concept and school achievement*. Englewood Cliffs, NJ: Prentice Hall.

Roderick, M. (1995). Grade retention and school dropout: Policy debate and research questions. *Research Bulletin*, No. 15. Bloomington, IN: Phi Delta Kappa Center for Evaluation, Development, and Research.

Schlechty, P. (1990). *Schools for the 21st century*. San Francisco: Jossey-Bass.

Schmoker, M. (1996). *Results*. Alexandria, VA: Association for Supervision and Curriculum Development.

Senge, P. (1990). *The fifth discipline*. New York: Doubleday.

Sensenbaugh, R. (1990). "Multiplicities of literacies in the 1990s." Eric Digest.

Sparks, D., & Hirsh, S. (1997). *A new vision for staff development*. Alexandria, VA: Association for Supervision and Curriculum Development.

Sparks, D., & Loucks-Horsley, S. (1989). "Five models of staff development." *Journal of Staff Development*, *10*(4), 1.

Spelling, M. (2005). "NAEP gains are elusive in key areas." *Education Week*, *25*(9), 22.

Tomlinson, C. (1999). *The differentiated classroom*. Alexandria, VA: Association for Supervision and Curriculum Development.

Vygotsky, L. (1991). *Thought and language* (5th ed.). England: Jossey-Bass.

Wheelock, A. (2002). *Using data to close achievement gap*. Thousand Oaks, CA: Corwin Press.

Franklin Pierce College Library

00165899